FIRST STEPS IN
EMBROIDERY

FIRST STEPS IN
EMBROIDERY

Introduced by Caroline Ollard

Macdonald Orbis

Acknowledgments

The photographs on the following pages are by courtesy of: Camera Press, London 12 – 13, 14, 15, 16, 17, 18, 35, 42, 44, 57; and J. & P. Coats, Edinburgh 8, 9.
The rest of the photographs were taken by the following photographers: Jan Baldwin, Tom Belshaw, Brian Boyle, Allan Grainger, Chris Harvey, Monique Leluhandre, Liz McAulay, Tino Tedaldi and Jerry Tubby.
The artwork was drawn by the following artists: Muriel Best, Amanda Bloom, Lindsay Blow, Sharon Finmark, Eugene Fleury, Suzanne Lisle, Coral Mula, Amanda Severne, Sue Sharples, Sheila Tizzard and Catherine Ward.

Front cover: Camera Press, London
Half title page: Jan Baldwin
Title page: Jan Baldwin
Back cover: Liz McAulay

A *Macdonald Orbis* BOOK

© Eaglemoss Publications Limited 1983, 1984

First published in Great Britain by
Orbis Publishing Limited, London 1985

Reprinted in 1987 by
Macdonald & Co (Publishers) Ltd
London & Sydney

A member of BPCC plc

This material previously appeared in the partwork
SuperStitch

Printed in Italy

ISBN: 0 356 14324 4

Macdonald & Co (Publishers) Ltd
Greater London House
Hampstead Road
London NW1 7QX

Contents

Introduction

It is the rich, worldwide tradition of embroidery which makes it such a fascinating craft. People have decorated fabrics with stitchery for centuries and embroidery is certainly one of the most ancient needlecrafts. From the glittering ceremonial robes of kings and queens to the everyday garments and household textiles of ordinary people, patterns and techniques have been created and passed on, right up to the present day.

Many historical embroideries were stitched by men. Hard to believe now, perhaps, but logical if you consider the early association of embroidery with religion and the predominantly male priesthoods. In medieval times 'professional' pieces of work took the form of beautiful pictorial embroideries, intricately worked using silk and metal threads. English examples were particularly prized, and the work was known in Europe as *Opus Anglicanum* – English work.

For women, embroidery has traditionally served as a pleasurable pastime. Since the Renaissance gentlewomen have practised embroidery as a refined activity, dedicated to producing virtuoso pieces of work, and the enthusiasm and output of Victorian ladies are still an inspiration.

Many of the designs given in this book have their roots in styles popular over the last few centuries. Some are treated traditionally, some are given a new look. One of the oldest techniques represented is blackwork, which came to sixteenth-century England from Spain and is based on Moorish patterns. Chapter 9 suggests an update for blackwork designs – in the kitchen!

The concept of the sampler – a library of stitches and patterns worked at home by a young girl as a kind of test piece – has been with us since the sixteenth century. Samplers come in all shapes and sizes, and chapter 5 offers a beautiful floral sampler picture. Crewel work, which became so popular on both sides of the Atlantic in the eighteenth century, appears in chapter 10, and a charming cushion cover echoes typical designs of the past with its flowing foliage outlined in stem and chain stitches with different fillings. Smocking, in contrast, is a traditionally English technique. Heavily decorated smocks were worn by men in rural areas during the eighteenth and nineteenth centuries, with many regional stitch and pattern variations. Start by experimenting with mock smocking before attempting the more traditional stitches; it is not as difficult as it looks.

Whitework, all-white stitchery on white fabric, has been popular in various forms throughout Europe since the Middle Ages. Chapter 11 provides a beautiful design in Mountmellick work, an Irish whitework which had its heyday in the nineteenth century. Delicate cutwork, another type of whitework, takes on a pastel tint in chapter 12: there's nothing to stop you departing from traditional colour schemes.

Embroidery stitches are numerous and it is impossible to cover them all in this book. However, *First Steps in Embroidery* contains all the well-known stitches, as well as some less familiar techniques. Each chapter introduces a new way of working, starting with the basic surface stitches. Looped and knotted stitches follow, in various simple and combined forms. From counted thread stitches and others which rely on neatness and regularity for their effect, you can progress to the more complex drawn thread, pulled thread and insertion stitches and the techniques of smocking, tambour bead-work and goldwork.

Clear step-by-step diagrams and simple instructions guide you through the various techniques. Working charts, trace patterns and diagrams provide all that is needed to complete both large and small projects. And full-colour photographs and drawings bring the work up close for you to see the detail.

You don't have to be a finicky perfectionist to enjoy this craft. Tiny stitches on fine fabric do make awe-inspiring heirlooms as we can see in pieces from the past, but with embroidery almost anything goes! Bold designs and vivid colours, chunky threads and fabrics all have their place. Needlecraft shops and departments are rich storehouses of threads of every possible hue – wools, cottons, silks, metallic threads and exciting extras like beads and sequins.

This book will guide you in your choice as well as your selection of equipment such as pins and needles, fabrics and frames. Each project has a comprehensive list of things you will need and discusses alternatives where applicable. Do not despair if you are miles from a needlecraft stockist. There are plenty of shops with mail-order services as well as specialist mail-order suppliers.

Embroidery can be used to decorate almost anything made from textiles. And if it is new ideas you are after, there is no shortage of those. Have you thought of embroidering a pretty border for a hand towel? Decorating a plain skirt with machine embroidery? Or adding a smocked collar and cuffs to a blouse?

The most precious gifts you can give are those that you have made yourself and many of the items in this book are perfect presents. Use the brilliantly coloured cross stitch alphabet to add a personal touch to almost anything. Stitch something beautiful for a baby or toddler, or choose one of the many items for the home. Start simply and complete a small project. The thrill of success will spur you on to greater things.

If you are a keen dressmaker, embroidery can add an extra dimension to garments. Discover how to embroider and make up a waistcoat, blouses, a skirt, a party dress, a glamorous scarf and a pair of exquisite little bags. All the projects can be made up by hand or machine, and your machine can play a part in the embroidery itself. Even a basic straight-stitch machine can cope with patterns and borders, and once you've tried out the techniques of freestyle swing-needle stitchery there's no end to the shimmering pictures you can create, beginning with the charming duck and drake from chapter 17.

The wide selection of designs and motifs can be used in other ways too. Watch out for the special Design Extra boxes. Their flashes of inspiration will set you on the road to adapting patterns and borders, picking out motifs, creating your own designs and using them to adorn any item you choose. For novice and expert alike, familiarity with the stitches and techniques in this book is the key which unlocks the door to a world of creativity – colours, textures, pictures and patterns at your fingertips. So start stitching now!

Caroline Ollard

Caroline Ollard, 1985

CHAPTER 1

Introducing materials and basic stitches

Embroidery covers a vast range of decorative skills using fabrics and threads of every kind. Once you have mastered even a few simple stitches, you have opened the door to a whole new world of creativity.

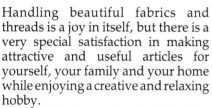

1 **2** **3**

Handling beautiful fabrics and threads is a joy in itself, but there is a very special satisfaction in making attractive and useful articles for yourself, your family and your home while enjoying a creative and relaxing hobby.

Much of the charm of embroidery lies in the fact that you need little equipment and there is hardly any setting out and clearing up to do. You are also working with textures and colours to produce your own unique combination of design, fabric, thread and technique. Embroidery is a surprisingly suitable hobby for people with a hectic lifestyle as the work can be picked up in odd moments – the problem is putting it down again!

It is always worth buying the best equipment – good quality tools are a

sound investment and a lasting pleasure to use.

Start with the most expensive item – a pair of small sharp embroidery scissors. You will also need a longer-bladed pair for cutting fabric, and an old pair for cutting paper.

Choose a smooth thimble to fit your middle finger, and buy a tape measure and a box of fine steel pins. Collect transparent plastic boxes (from haberdashers) for storing threads, and find a needlebook or piece of flannel for your needles.

Threads

Many threads both natural and man-made are manufactured especially for embroidery. You can also incorporate knitting and weaving yarns, metal threads or raffia.

Choosing and using thread Keep in mind the intended use for the embroidery. Does it need to be washed or dry-cleaned? Will it have to stand up to a lot of wear.

Choose threads accordingly, noticing the differences between them – thin or thick, twisted or loose. Bear in mind the contrast between the thread and the background – shiny threads show up against a dull background.

Don't use too long a thread in the needle. 50cm/20in is enough for most purposes. If a thread wears thin or fluffs up, replace it immediately with a fresh length. You will often find you need to use only a few strands of the total thickness of some threads. Separate the strands carefully – rub the ends of the required strands and pull gently to avoid tangles.

Four basic stitches

Straight stitch

This is a single stitch, made in any direction. Straight stitches can be grouped in geometric shapes, used in lines, scattered about singly or with other stitches, or used to make broad effects like brush strokes.

Back stitch

Work from right to left. Bring the needle up a stitch away from the beginning of the line, take a stitch an equal distance behind and in front. Pull thread through. For the next stitch the needle goes down where it first came up.

Stem stitch

Work from left to right, or upwards. Take a long stitch forward and a shorter, slanting stitch back. The more pronounced the slant, the thicker the line. Keep the thread under the needle.

Chain stitch

Work from right to left, or downwards. Bring the thread out at the beginning of the line, hold the thread down with the left thumb while the needle is reinserted into the same spot and brought out again a short distance away. Draw it through over the loop of thread under your thumb. The needle always goes down again into the same hole.

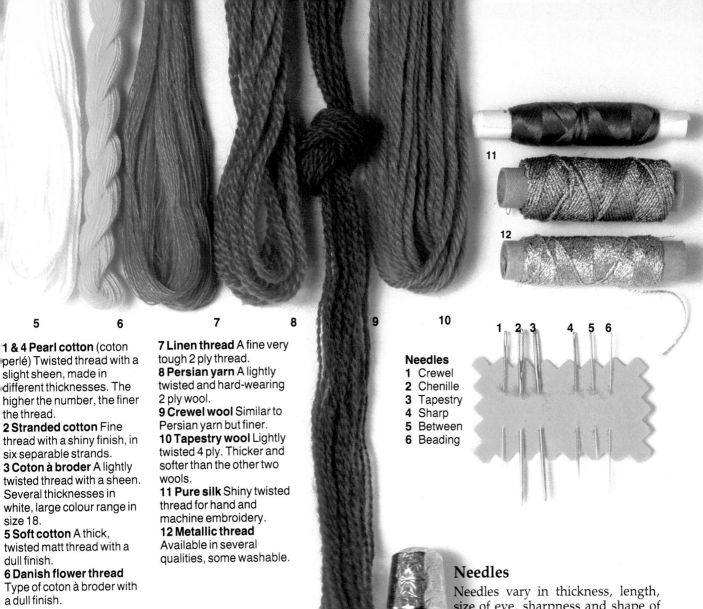

| 5 | 6 | 7 | 8 | 9 | 10 |

1 & 4 Pearl cotton (coton perlé) Twisted thread with a slight sheen, made in different thicknesses. The higher the number, the finer the thread.

2 Stranded cotton Fine thread with a shiny finish, in six separable strands.

3 Coton à broder A lightly twisted thread with a sheen. Several thicknesses in white, large colour range in size 18.

5 Soft cotton A thick, twisted matt thread with a dull finish.

6 Danish flower thread Type of coton à broder with a dull finish.

7 Linen thread A fine very tough 2 ply thread.

8 Persian yarn A lightly twisted and hard-wearing 2 ply wool.

9 Crewel wool Similar to Persian yarn but finer.

10 Tapestry wool Lightly twisted 4 ply. Thicker and softer than the other two wools.

11 Pure silk Shiny twisted thread for hand and machine embroidery.

12 Metallic thread Available in several qualities, some washable.

Needles
1 Crewel
2 Chenille
3 Tapestry
4 Sharp
5 Between
6 Beading

Needles

Needles vary in thickness, length, size of eye, sharpness and shape of point, depending on the fabric and type of stitchery. A number indicates the size: the higher the number, the finer the needle.

Crewel The basic all-round embroidery needle, with a fine point and a long eye to take several strands of thread. A packet of sizes 5-10 covers most types of surface stitchery on closely woven fabric.

Chenille A bigger needle with a large eye for thick threads and a sharp point. It is useful for taking couched threads to the back of the fabric.

Tapestry A blunt needle with a large eye. It is inserted between the threads of the fabric without piercing them. Used for needlepoint and counted thread work such as cross stitch, pulled and drawn thread work, and lacing on composite stitches.

Sharp A general sewing needle with a small eye.

Between Same as sharp, but shorter. It is a favourite quilting needle.

Beading A long, very fine needle with a tiny eye for small beads.

Two chain stitch variations

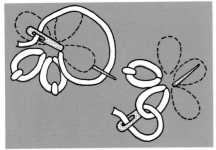

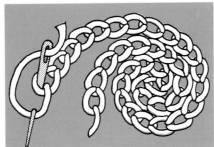

Detached chain stitch

This is also often called lazy daisy stitch as it is suitable for forming daisy-like flower motifs. Work a chain stitch in the normal way, but instead of reinserting the needle to form a second stitch, make a small stitch to catch down the loop of the first one and hold it in place. Work these in a circle for 'flowers' or separately for other effects.

Chain filling

Work the chain stitch in a line, but in a circular direction from the centre outwards, so that a solid round stitched area forms. This is useful for floral and other circle-based motifs.

9

Frames

A frame is not essential, but many stitches are easier to work on taut fabric, as they keep an even tension and there is no fear of puckering. If you use a frame, you work each stitch in two separate movements – right through the fabric to the back of the work and then out to the front again. (Stitches on hand-held work can be made in one action – the needle picks up successive stitch lengths of fabric.) Some frames come with table or floor stands so that you have both hands free for embroidery. The simplest type of frame for surface embroidery is the ring frame; others such as the rectangular slate frame are dealt with in chapter 5, page 24.

Ring frames come in various sizes,

measured by diameter, ranging from 7.5cm–30cm/3in–12in. They are suitable for working small designs and should be big enough to encompass the complete design.

Framing up Separate the two hoops.
1 Bind the inner ring with soft hem tape or bias strips of torn fabric. This stops your base fabric from slipping.
2 Lay the fabric over the inner ring, right side up, and press the outer ring in place.
Adjust the fabric evenly before tightening the screw.
If you need to move the ring along to a new area of fabric, protect the stitches already worked with a spare piece of soft fabric laid over the base fabric and cut away above the area you wish to work.

How to transfer designs

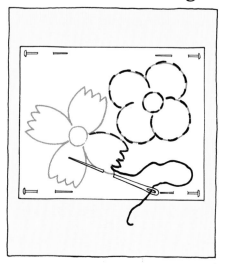

There are several ways to transfer embroidery designs on to fabric. Everyone has a favourite method, although often one method will be more suitable than another.

Trace and tack

This method will transfer a design on to most fabrics, and as it leaves no mark, the design can easily be altered.
Trace off the design on to tissue or tracing paper.
Lay the tracing on the right side of the fabric and pin in place. Outline the design with small running stitches through both paper and fabric.
Run the needle point along the lines of stitching to cut the tissue and tear it away carefully.

Dressmaker's carbon

This quick and easy method is suitable for marking designs on to smooth fabrics. The special carbon paper is available in several colours. Use a pale one for dark fabrics. Simply pin your traced design over the fabric with a sheet of dressmaker's carbon slipped in between, carbon side down. Then trace over the lines of the design with a fairly pointed implement such as a ballpoint with its cap on. For simple geometric designs, you could use a tracing wheel – a serrated-edged wheel mounted on a handle. The outline of the motif will appear on the fabric as a dotted line.

Window method

A simple motif can be traced directly on to most pale fabrics if both design and fabric are held up to the light as follows:
Trace off the design in bold black lines on to a piece of tracing paper and tape the tracing to a window pane with adhesive tape.
Then tape the fabric firmly in position over the tracing and trace the design on to the fabric using a sharp 2H pencil or a washable embroidery marker. (The marker can easily be sponged off if necessary.) Make sure the fabric is taut and positioned correctly over the traced design.

A pocketful of flowers

Breathe new life into a plain shirt with this fresh and pretty design of cornfield flowers. Work the motif in basic stitches on to a white or plain-coloured shirt with a breast pocket from which the flowers will appear to spring.

You will need

One skein each Coats Anchor stranded cotton in greens 0238 and 0267, red 046, blue 0132, yellow 0305 and black 0403

Crewel needle size 8 or 9

Tracing paper and tacking thread or dressmaker's carbon paper

Small ring frame if possible

Working the design

If you are using a new shirt, wash it first so that it does not shrink later and pucker your stitches.

If possible, mount the area to be worked on a ring frame. Thread the needle with three strands of the cotton. Don't knot it, but begin with some tiny neat back stitches which you will then cover up with your embroidery.

Work the cornflowers in straight rows of chain stitch sewn from the centre outwards. The poppy is worked in chain stitch filling, with the flower outlined and then filled in.

Use the trace design below for the flowers on the shirt above. Transfer it using one of the methods already described.

Next work the yellow corn in detached chain stitch and make your straight catching stitches long enough to look like the whiskers on the ears of corn. Use detached chain stitch again to work the black centre of the poppy. Then sew the bright green grass in stem stitch and the darker green stems in back stitch. The poppy bud is worked in green chain stitch and red straight stitches. At the lower edge of the design, extend your stitches 6mm/¼in inside the pocket.

Finishing off

Finish threads off by working a few small stitches in the back of the work and snipping off. Make sure the wrong side is neat and that you have not carried thread across white areas where it will show through on the right side.

11

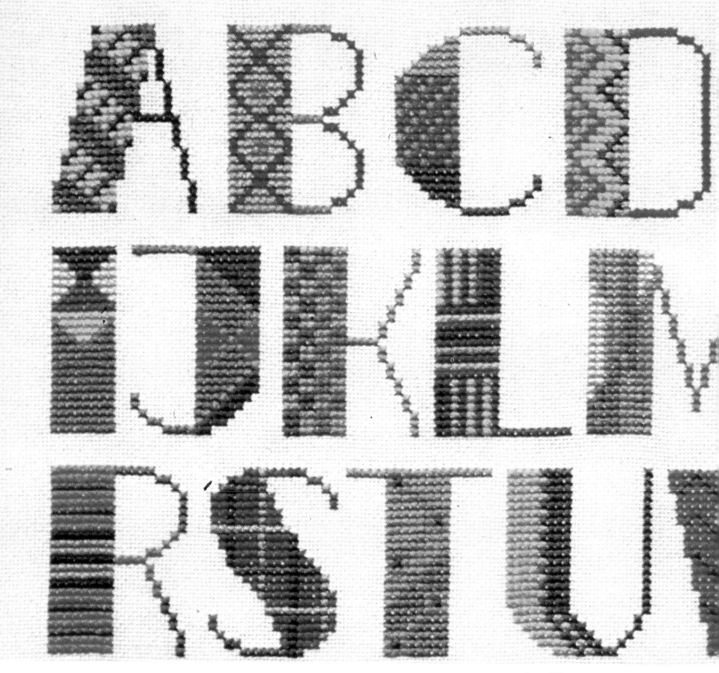

CHAPTER 2
Creative cross stitch

Cross stitch is the basis for traditional embroidery throughout much of the world, but it is also effective in contemporary work like these bold, bright letters. Stitch an initial – or sew the whole colourful alphabet.

Universally popular in Europe, particularly in Scandinavia and the Slav countries, cross stitch designs and motifs have been passed down with traditional folklore and every country has its own characteristic colours. It is one of the easiest of stitches – based on a single diagonal stitch made first in one direction and then in another to cross the first at right angles. These crosses are worked in groups to form strong blocks of colour, or else in lines to create outlines, letters and numerals.

Counted thread embroidery

Cross stitch is one of many stitches that are worked over counted threads – that is, the threads of the fabric are used to place the stitches. Evenweave fabric with regular, identical numbers of threads across both the warp and the weft is used. It comes in several weaves, from fine to coarse, ranging from ten to thirty threads to 2.5cm/1in. The size of stitch, and consequently of motif, depends on how many threads you are working over. The overall shape of

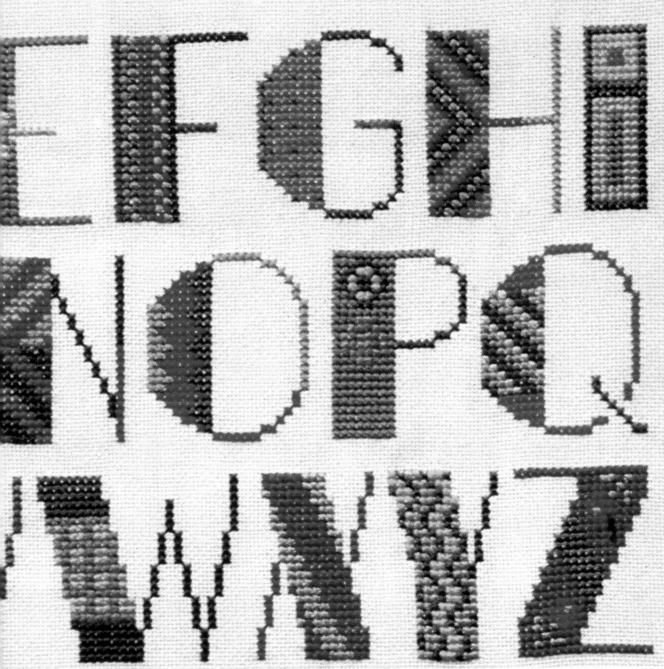

cross stitches should be square, covering the same number of threads vertically and horizontally. If you were to use a fabric of uneven weave, the stitches would be distorted.

Cross stitch can be sewn in many different scales, depending on the thread and fabric used, and the design being embroidered. To make a design larger, use a fabric with fewer threads to 2.5cm/1in and make larger crosses using thicker thread. Or, use more strands over more threads of the same fabric. To make a design smaller, reverse either of these processes.

Fabrics The most suitable fabric for cross stitch is an evenweave. Choose one where you can see clearly

Sizing up your cross stitch

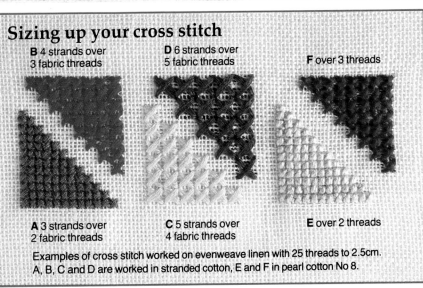

B 4 strands over 3 fabric threads

D 6 strands over 5 fabric threads

F over 3 threads

A 3 strands over 2 fabric threads

C 5 strands over 4 fabric threads

E over 2 threads

Examples of cross stitch worked on evenweave linen with 25 threads to 2.5cm. A, B, C and D are worked in stranded cotton, E and F in pearl cotton No 8.

enough to count the threads. Gingham and other checked fabrics are also convenient, as the stitch 'squares' are already marked out. (Make sure the needle goes into the same hole at each corner.)

Needles Use a blunt tapestry needle with a large eye, size 20 to 24 depending on the weave of the fabric.

Threads Many embroidery threads are suitable for cross stitch, particularly stranded cotton, coton à broder, Danish flower thread, No 8 pearl cotton and soft cotton. Pearl cotton is twisted and lustrous, and gives a particularly bold effect. At the coarser

end of the fabric scale, try crewel wool, or stranded Persian yarn on evenweave wool.

How to begin
Unlike freestyle embroidery designs, which are worked over a marked outline, no tracing is needed, although iron-on transfers marked out in crosses are available. Cross stitch is usually worked from a chart where each square denotes one cross stitch. You can work in horizontal rows, or in separate stitches, depending on the design.

When working in rows, lay down one set of diagonal threads first, then

add the crossing threads. For neatness, all the upper threads must lie in the same direction on one piece of work, unless you particularly wish to emphasize part of the design by the light catching threads running in the opposite direction.

Calculating the size of a design If you are working cross stitch from a chart, it is often hard to visualize the size of a finished design before you begin working it. This simple method of calculating the dimensions will save a few mistakes.

Work a 2cm/¾in row of cross stitches on the fabric. Count the

Working basic cross stitch

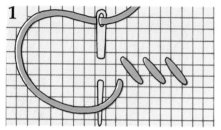 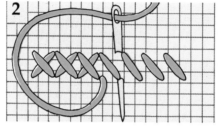 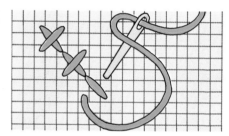

To work horizontally
Working over two threads:
1 Bring the needle up on the right-hand side of the row at the bottom. Re-insert it two threads to the left and two threads up to form a diagonal half-cross. Bring the needle up again two threads along from where it first came up, and

continue along the row.
2 Work the upper crossing stitches by reversing the process and working from left to right. Bring the needle up on the left-hand side at the bottom. The needle should go through the same holes as on the first row, and the back of the work should have even vertical stitches.

To work diagonally
When working isolated stitches, or diagonal or vertical rows of a particular colour, it is easier to work individual complete crosses before passing on to the next stitch.

Below: Embroider initials on to a tiny bag and trim with twisted threads.

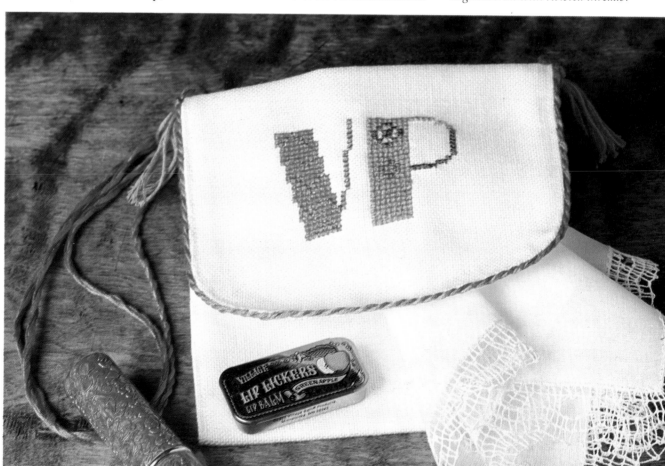

stitches. Now count the number of crosses on the chart in the length and width of the design to be copied. Divide each of these figures by the number of crosses in 2cm/¾in. Double each total to get the finished length and width of the stitched design for your particular fabric.

For example, a chart of 40 crosses long and 20 crosses wide on fabric with 10 crosses to 2cm/¾in will produce a design 8cm×4cm/6¼in× 1½in. On fabric with 5 crosses to 2cm/¾in this design measures 16cm× 8cm/6¼in×3¼in.

Cross stitch on fine fabrics

To work a cross stitch design on an uneven or close weave, or a very fine fabric such as organdie, tack a piece of fine, single thread canvas over the area to be worked. Sew the cross stitches over the canvas, pulling fairly tightly to avoid loose stitches later, and carefully cut the canvas close to the motif.

Pull away the canvas threads. It is best to remove all the threads running in one direction first.

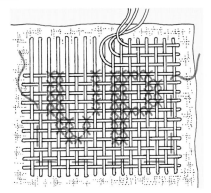

Colourful alphabet in cross stitch

Personalize a present with one, two or several of the brilliantly coloured letters on pages 12 and 13. They could find a home on many different items – pin cushions, needlecases, tops of trinket boxes or tiny bedroom cushions. You could stitch your favourite child's name and frame it, or for a beautiful nursery sampler picture, sew the whole alphabet, using the large picture as a layout guide. Or, using a piece of fine canvas as described above, stitch a name or initial on to T-shirts, sweatshirts, towels, dungarees or baby clothes. The letters are worked entirely in cross stitch using stranded cotton thread in a range of glowing colours. You can use the shades in the picture or choose your own. The colour of the

background fabric should complement the bright colours. Each letter will be about 4.5cm/1¾in high when finished, but you can make them as large or as small as you like by changing the base fabric and thread.

You will need

Coats Anchor stranded cotton in at least four different shades
Evenweave fabric, 25 threads to 2.5cm/1in
Tapestry needle size 22 or 24
Small embroidery hoop if possible

Stitching the letters

Each letter includes a solid, multi-coloured area, and some plain lines. Work the cross stitches over two threads of the fabric using three

strands of thread.

The big picture is your working guide for the colours and patterns. Charts are given below for the first three letters of the alphabet to show you how the patterns are built up. Work in horizontal rows where practical, turning the embroidery 90 degrees to work along the length of some of the letters; otherwise work vertically, or diagonally, in separate single stitches. Remember to work all the crossing threads in the same direction.

If more than one letter is to be worked, do not carry threads across on the wrong side; finish them off and start a new length for the next letter. Letters should be at least four fabric threads apart.

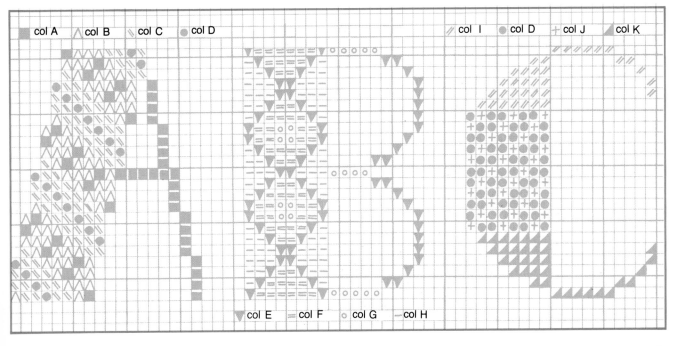

col A   col B   col C   col D

col I   col D   col J   col K

col E   col F   col G   col H

CHAPTER 3

Shimmering satin stitch

Satin stitch is beautifully smooth and glossy. It is useful for working many different kinds of motifs.
A swarm of honey bees has settled on this lovely bright table linen – learn basic satin stitch and French knots, and you will find them simple to embroider.

Satin stitch is a very commonly used stitch in embroidery, and is ideal for filling in solid areas of colour. Some preliminary practice will help you to get your stitches lying neatly side by side to obtain the silky finish which gives the stitch its name.

Working hints

All the stitches in each design, or part of a design, should lie in the same direction. The direction you choose will have quite an effect on the finished work because of the way the stitching catches the light. The stitch can be worked effectively and neatly on evenweave fabric.

When working satin stitch, always make sure the ends of the stitches cover any outlines marked on the base fabric, and make a clean edge. Always work with a frame to avoid drawing up the base fabric and keep all the stitches at the same tension so that there is no puckering when the frame is removed. If the motif is too large for a single row of satin stitches, use several rows worked neatly end to end or use encroaching satin stitch.

Below: These embroidered bees could be worked on any bright cotton fabric to match your kitchen colour scheme.

Three useful stitches

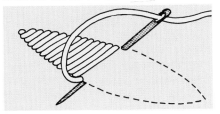

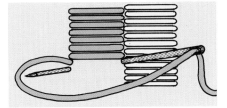

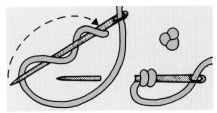

Satin stitch
Make a series of straight stitches lying close to each other. Bring the needle up and re-insert it on the other side of the motif being worked; bring the needle up again very close to where it first went in, being careful not to pull the first stitch too tight. Continue across the motif in this way.

Encroaching satin stitch
When you need more than one row of satin stitch to cover an area, you can work the ends of the second row stitches between the ends of the stitches on the first row. The two rows will blend together smoothly. Encroaching satin stitch is often used for subtle tone variations in the shade of the thread.

French knots
Bring the needle out where you want to make the stitch. Anchor the thread with your free thumb and circle the needle point twice round the thread. Keeping the thread anchored, re-insert the needle close to where it came up. Carefully pull it through to catch the knot down. Begin working next knot or secure with a backstitch.

Honey bee tablewear

The warm, honey-yellow gingham used to make this tablewear and matching apron is the perfect background for lively bees worked in simple embroidery stitches. Alternatively, you can use plain or striped fabric.

Placemat and napkin

The bee motifs make an attractive and inviting place setting when stitched on to a placemat and matching napkin. Use a bought mat and napkin, or make them up yourself.

You will need
For one placemat and one napkin (to work 23 to 25 bees)
Coats Anchor stranded cotton: 2 skeins black 0403, 1 skein each yellow 0298, grey 0398, green 0225
40cm/½yd of fabric (90cm/36in wide)
To work either one mat *or* one napkin: 1 skein in each shade
Tracing paper and dressmaker's carbon
Crewel needle

Working the mat and napkin
If you are making up your own table linen, work the embroidery first. Trace off bees of different sizes from the patterns overleaf on to tracing paper. Using dressmaker's carbon paper and a ball-point with its cap on, transfer as many bees as you want to the opposing corners of a rectangular piece of gingham fabric or on to a bought placemat. Position the bees at random wherever

you want them, or use the picture (below) as a guide. They should be at least 2cm/¾in away from edge of fabric if you are making your own mat. For the napkin, trace some different bees on to one corner of a square napkin, again making sure they are at least 2cm/¾in away from the edge of the fabric if making your own.
Mount the fabric in a ring frame (see the Professional Touch overleaf). With three strands of thread in the needle, work each bee's head in satin stitch so that stitches lie from head to tail. Add alternating yellow and black stripes for the body, using encroaching satin stitch to suggest softness.
Outline the end part of the body in black stem stitch. Use grey stem stitch for the wings, black for the legs, add black backstitched antennae and green French knots for the eyes.

Below: A matching mat and napkin set.

Tea-cosy

This tea-cosy really does look cosy. Shaped like beehives with embroidered bees buzzing round the entrances, both tea and egg-cosies are filled with wadding to keep your boiled egg and teapot snug. Make up your own simple cosies using fabric on which you have already embroidered the bees and the hive entrances. The outer seams are finished with a neat trim of bias binding.

You will need

For 1 tea-cosy, to work 15 bees and the hive entrance, Coats Anchor stranded cotton: 2 skeins black 0403, 1 skein each yellow 0298, grey 0398 and green 0225
Tracing paper and dressmaker's carbon
Crewel needle
40cm/½yd polyester wadding (8oz)
70cm/¾yd of fabric (90cm/36in wide or more) depending on size of teapot
1.50–2m/1½–2yd matching bias binding (25mm/1in wide)

Working the tea-cosy

Measure your teapot (or coffee pot if you prefer). Make up a standard tea-cosy pattern, and mark on to the fabric the outline of the two cosy pieces and the position of the bees and hive entrance. The hive entrance should be in the centre of the cosy, about 1cm/½in from the lower foldline of the cosy front. Embroider the motifs and then cut out the cosy. Fold the two pieces in half with wadding sandwiched in the middle, and tack it in place. Add about 12 horizontal lines of machine stitching through all layers. If you use gingham, follow the rows of checks to keep the lines straight, making bands of decreasing width to look like a beehive (see photograph on pages 16 and 17). When you come to an embroidered motif, interrupt the line of stitching.
Place the front and back of the cosy wrong sides together and stitch, finishing the seam with bias binding.

Egg-cosy

This charming egg-cosy is simple and quick to make. Adorned with just one bee, it makes a perfect small gift.

You will need

Coats Anchor stranded cotton:
1 skein each of colours as for tea-cosy
Tracing paper and dressmaker's carbon
Crewel needle
20cm/¼yd polyester wadding (4oz)
20cm/¼yd fabric (90cm/36in wide)
40cm/½yd matching bias binding (25mm/1in wide)

Working the egg-cosy

The working method for the egg-cosy is similar to that for the tea-cosy, except that a lighter wadding is used. Follow the pattern (right) for the shape of the cosy. The pattern also shows you the position of the bee, hive entrance, machine-stitched rows, and bias-bound edging.

Apron

Honey bees are buzzing contentedly across the bib and pocket of the gingham apron. Use a bought apron, or make up a simple one with a neck-strap, waist ties, and gathered skirt. If you are making your own apron, embroider the pocket and bib piece first. The bee motifs are transferred and worked in exactly the same way as for the mats and napkins on the previous page.

You will need

For the embroidery:
Bought or made-up apron
To embroider 11–15 bees, Coats Anchor stranded cotton: 2 skeins black 0403, 1 skein each yellow 0298, grey 0398 and green 0225
Tracing paper and dressmaker's carbon
Crewel needle

If making your own apron, you will need 120cm/1⅜yd of 90cm/36in wide fabric and 110cm/1¼yd of 25mm/1in wide matching bias binding for the edging.

Left: The bib of an apron provides an effective area for embroidery and a toning border sets the bees off well.

Framing tricky corners

To embroider right into the corner of a napkin, mat or handkerchief, attach the work to a backing fabric but cut away the area behind the embroidery.

Lay a piece of firm cotton fabric over the inner ring of your ring frame (a piece of old sheet will do). Place the corner to be worked on top.

Press the outer ring in place. Work herringbone stitches round the edges of the corner, keeping both fabrics taut. Tack round the embroidery area, turn the hoop over, and carefully cut away the backing fabric within the tacking. When the work is completed, take it out of the frame and unpick the remainder of the backing fabric.

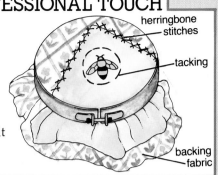

Trace patterns for bee motifs

These patterns are the right size for tracing and transferring to the fabric using dressmaker's carbon paper.

19

CHAPTER 4

Blanket and buttonhole stitch

Blanket stitch and its close relation, the more delicate buttonhole stitch, are traditional edging stitches. Apart from their obvious practical function, they can also be put to good decorative use. It's worth learning to work them neatly to get the best value from their versatility.

Blanket stitch is so called because it is a traditional edging for woollen blankets.

Blanket stitch *is* a good edging, particularly for non-woven fabrics such as felt, but can be worked just as well in the centre of a piece of fabric. The stitches can be used as motif outlines or straight lines – even as filling stitches. Delicate, feathery effects are possible, as well as bold, bright designs.

Basic stitch techniques

Like chain stitch, both belong to the family of stitches called looped stitches, where a loop is formed on the surface of the base fabric, and caught in place by another stitch.

Blanket stitches are worked a little way apart from one another, whereas buttonhole stitch is worked closely together and usually on a smaller scale – otherwise the two stitches are formed in exactly the same way.

Work blanket and buttonhole stitches evenly for a neat appearance with regularly spaced stitches of identical length. They are all suitable for evenweave fabrics, whose regular threads can help you to work tidily.

Left: This multi-coloured embroidery includes blanket stitch edging and traditional peasant-style motifs.

Enlarging and reducing

Successful embroidery can often depend on an accurate, well-marked design. Motifs, borders or pictures taken from books or prints may need to be enlarged or reduced according to the work in hand. A good method is to first mark the design with a squared grid. Then copy the design on to a grid of larger or smaller squares to make it larger or smaller. Use this method also for enlarging pattern pieces given on squared graphs.

To enlarge Make a tracing of the design and, using a ruler, mark a square or oblong frame closely

Blanket stitch

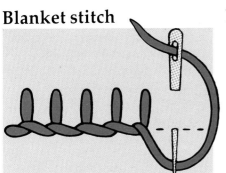

Work from left to right making every stitch the same height. Bring the needle out on the bottom line. If working the stitch as an edging, secure the thread underneath a little way in from the edge, and bring to the front.
Re-insert the needle on the top line, slightly to the right, and bring it out again directly underneath, on the bottom line. Pull the stitch through with the thread under the needle point to catch the loop.
Keep tension even throughout – do not pull any of the stitches too tight.

Buttonhole stitch

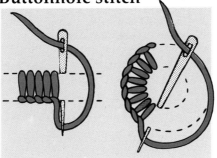

This stitch is worked in exactly the same way as blanket stitch, except that when you re-insert the needle on the top line, it should be close to the previous stitch.
Work all subsequent stitches very close together to form a smooth band.
Keep the stitches the same height, taking special care when working in curves or scallops.
Buttonhole wheels Work a tight circle of buttonhole stitch (caught loops on the outside) to form a useful round motif of any size.

Closed buttonhole stitch

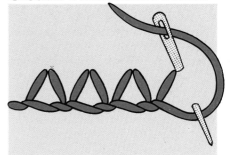

This buttonhole stitch variation is a very practical and attractive edging stitch and forms a triangular pattern.
Bring the needle out on the bottom line and re-insert it on the top line, slightly to the right. Bring it out again next to where it first came out (bottom line) and pull through, catching the loop under the point of the needle. Now re-insert on the top line, next to end of last stitch and bring the needle out on the bottom line, slightly to the right. Pull through, catching the loop.

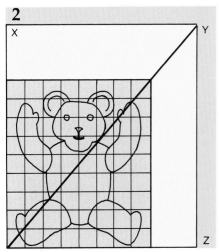

round it.
Mark this area off in regular squares – a simple method is to stick the tracing over a piece of graph paper.
1 Place the squared design in the bottom left-hand corner of a large sheet of paper. Draw a diagonal line from the bottom left to the top right-hand corner, and extend it on to the paper underneath.
2 On the plain paper, mark the level of the desired height for the design and extend the left-hand frame edge up to this height, X. Draw a horizontal line from X to cut the diagonal line at Y. From Y, draw a

downward vertical line as far as the bottom line (which should be extended to Z). You now have a scaled-up frame for the larger design. Remove the original design.
3 Mark the new large square or oblong off into the same number of squares as the small one. The squares will be proportionately larger.
Carefully copy the design, square by square, on to the large grid.
It is helpful to first mark where the main design lines intersect grid lines.

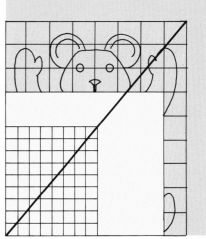

To reduce Use the same process in reverse to make a design smaller. Place a small sheet of paper in the lower left-hand corner of the squared-off large design and join opposite corners of the design to obtain the diagonal line. Decide on the new height and mark the top right-hand corner of the new grid. Join this point to the bottom and side lines.
Divide the area obtained into the same number of squares as the larger design and copy the design on to this small grid in the same way as for enlarging.

21

Peasant-style waistcoat for a child

This beautiful waistcoat made for a 6 to 8 year old (70cm/28in chest) is made up in a warm black fabric to show the bright embroidery yarn to best advantage. Work the embroidery in your hand – do not use a ring frame. There's no need to turn in the waistcoat edges – simply finish with blanket stitch.
The design is embroidered in blanket stitch and chain stitch with a little satin stitch. Traditionally, this type of design was worked in one colour on smocks, usually in the same colour as the base fabric. In the 1920s it was taken up by Dorset women who called it 'Dorset feather stitchery'. They used buttonhole or blanket stitch almost exclusively, but the chain stitch added here complements it perfectly.

You will need
40cm/16in black woollen coating fabric or blanketing (90cm/36in or wider) – non-woven fabrics are the most suitable
2 skeins each Coats Anchor stranded wool in red T3559, blue T3323, yellow T3535, 1 skein green T3507
Chenille needle size 2
Fine sewing needle and black polyester thread for making up
Tracing paper and coloured pens

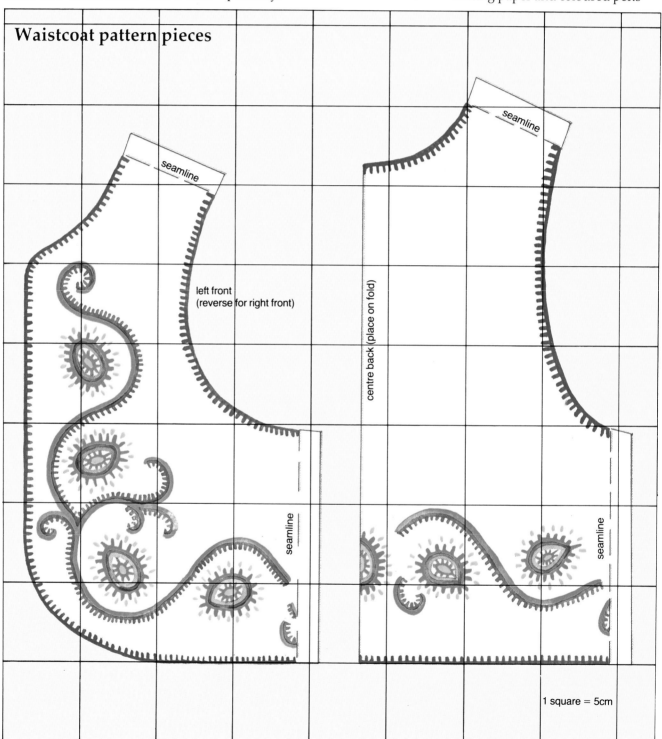

Waistcoat pattern pieces

left front
(reverse for right front)

seamline

centre back (place on fold)

seamline

seamline

1 square = 5cm

Preparing the waistcoat pieces

Enlarge the waistcoat pattern pieces and embroidery design as described on pages 20–21. Use squared dressmaker's graph paper for the enlarging (one square on chart = 5cm/2in), and then cut the pieces out in tracing paper – right and left fronts and a complete back. Mark shoulder and side seamlines. Mark the main lines of the embroidery design given for the left front and left half of the back on to the pattern pieces, using coloured felt-tips. (There is no need to mark any of the yellow parts of the design.) Reverse left front to trace design on right front. Fold back piece down centre back to trace design on to right half of back.

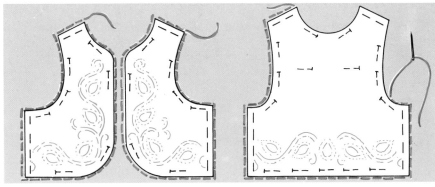

Transferring the design

Pin the three tracing paper pieces to the fabric, leaving ample space between them, particularly at side and shoulders. Tack along pattern cutting lines, then along main design lines of motifs. When the whole pattern is tacked in place, tear away the tracing paper, making sure all the tacking threads remain intact. Mark side and shoulder seamlines with tailor's chalk.

Working the design

The embroidery will be easier to work if you now cut the fabric into three separate pieces. Do not cut along final cutting lines, as the fabric may fray. Instead, cut the pieces out with about 1cm to spare all round.

With two strands of yarn in the needle, work the design in colours and stitches as shown. Use yarn in lengths of not more than 35cm/14in. Work the blanket stitch first, then the chain stitch, and finally the satin stitch and the yellow lazy daisies. Do not pull the stitches too tight. Remove tacking stitches.

Keep the wrong side of the work as neat as possible. Stop stitching about 1cm/½in short of the little red and blue 'curl' motif which comes over the side seam.

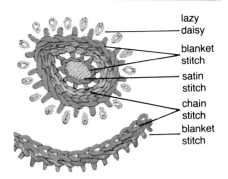

Joining seams

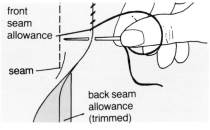

When all the embroidery except that at the side seams is done, cut along the side seam cutting lines and sew the side seams by hand or by machine. Trim the back seam allowance only to 1cm/½in and fold front seam allowance over it; secure with neat hemming stitches. Join shoulder seams in the same way. Now work the rest of the design over the side seams.

Above: The embroidery appears on the back of the waistcoat too. If you prefer, work the blanket stitch edging only.

Working the edging

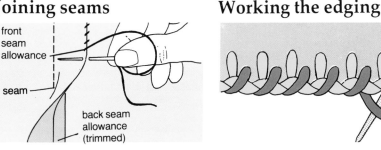

Cut out the armholes along tacked cutting lines and remove any remaining tacking. Follow colour chart, work blanket stitch round armhole edges. With four strands of contrast yarn in the needle, 'whip' the blanket stitch, catching in a little of the fabric between each blanket stitch to prevent fraying and give a secure edge to the waistcoat. (A whipping stitch is one that overcasts another stitch to make it more decorative. It does not always pass through the ground fabric.)

Now cut the lower, front and neck edges along cutting lines and work the border in the same way.

CHAPTER 5

Six new sampler stitches

*Building up your repertoire of new embroidery stitches is
exciting – especially when you can use
them right away in a sampler picture. Add them to the basic
stitches you already know and work pictorial
subjects such as this elegant bowl of flowers.*

This chapter shows you how to work two knotted stitches, two flat stitches, and two looped stitches, all of which are particularly rewarding to work. Bullion knots, for instance, are

slightly trickier than French knots but look most effective when worked correctly.
Coral stitch is a quick knotted line stitch. Fishbone stitch gives a close,

flat effect, useful for working leaves and petals, while herringbone stitch can be worked closely or widely spaced according to the motif. Fly stitch and feather stitch are also versatile and decorative. Notice the different effects of working fly stitch singly, as an all-over stitch, or in rows. It is a good idea, when trying out new stitches, to practise first on a spare piece of fabric.

Right: Floral pictures have a universal appeal and this lovely embroidered version would be equally at home in a traditional or contemporary setting.

Rectangular embroidery frames

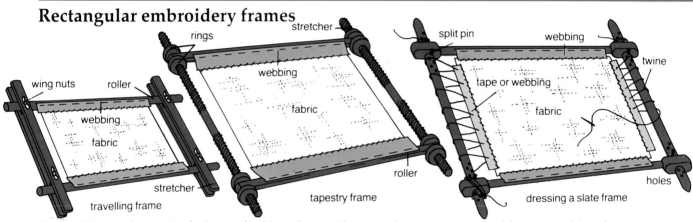

For medium or large-sized pieces of embroidery such as the picture (right) you will need a more substantial frame than a ring frame. There are three kinds of rectangular frame – the travelling (or rotating) frame, the tapestry frame, and the slate frame. Each has a roller, with webbing attached at the top and bottom. On all three the fabric is stretched in the same way, but they have different stretchers.
For beginners, the tapestry frame is a good choice. Try to buy one with its own stand.
Travelling frame The stretchers on this frame have a slot at each end and tension is produced by turning the rollers. Although it is of a convenient size – smaller than the other two types – it is difficult to achieve a good tension on it, especially with canvas.
Tapestry frame This has longer stretchers, with a thread. To obtain the tension, rings are screwed along them above and below each roller. The fabric used must be more than half the length of the stretchers. This popular frame can be bought with a table or floor stand.

Slate frame The stretchers are two pierced slats, which are inserted through slots in the rollers. To tension the fabric, split pins are inserted through holes in the slats, keeping the rollers apart. Slate frames are available with floor stands, which release both hands for working all the time.

Dressing a rectangular frame
The method of mounting light and heavy fabrics on a rectangular or square frame is slightly different. Light fabrics are best mounted on to calico first. Framing light fabrics is described on page 34.

Medium to heavy fabrics
Cut the fabric carefully along the grain to at least 5cm/2in larger than the desired finished size on each side. Find the centre points of the top and bottom edges and mark them. Make permanent marks with a laundry marker at the centre of the webbing on each roller.
Turn under a 5mm/¼in single hem at the top of the fabric and press. Lay it on the right side of the

webbing, matching the centre marks, and pin it to the webbing from the centre outwards, stretching it as you go. Oversew it to the webbing with strong thread and remove the pins. Attach the opposite edge to the other roller in the same way.
Now fit the rollers and stretchers together, making the necessary adjustments to ensure that the fabric is kept absolutely taut. Reinforce the side edges by overcasting pieces of cotton tape or webbing over them. Tie a length of fine upholstery twine to one end of the right-hand stretcher. Using a large needle, lash the edge of the fabric to the stretcher by passing the twine through the tape and fabric and round the stretcher. Wind the twine several times round the end of the stretcher.
Lash the fabric to the left-hand stretcher in the same way. When you have finished, the fabric should be as tight as a drum. If it slackens during working, the rollers may be adjusted and the twine can be unwound and pulled tight again.

Bowl of flowers embroidered picture

Samplers do not have to be confined to cross stitch and alphabets. This one includes all the new stitches shown in this chapter, plus some which you will have used already. The design has a lovely flat, stencil-like quality. The use of voided (un-stitched) areas makes it even more effective and less time consuming. The picture area measures 33cm× 43cm/13in×17in.

You will need
50cm/½yd cream embroidery fabric
  (medium-weight linen or similar)
1 skein each DMC stranded cotton
  in 783 (gold) and 919 (dark
  terracotta)
2 skeins in 597 (blue-green)
3 skeins in 921 (light terracotta)
1 skein each DMC pearl cotton in
  783, 919, 921 and 597
Greaseproof or tracing paper
Dressmaker's carbon paper
Pencil and ball-point pen
Rectangular embroidery frame
Crewel needles size 6

Transferring the design
Trace the main design outlines from the trace pattern on to the greaseproof or tracing paper.
Cut the linen to a rectangle at least 43cm×53cm/17in×21in. Press to remove any creases and lay on a flat surface. Place the carbon paper over the linen and pin the tracing centrally over the top.
Draw firmly over the main design lines, using a ball-point pen, to transfer the design to the fabric. Remove the tracing and carbon paper. If any parts of the design have not transferred clearly, go over them with a hard, sharp pencil.

Working the design
Mount the piece of fabric on the embroidery frame. Following the stitch guide, work the design in colours and threads as specified, using three strands of stranded cotton in the needle, and one of pearl cotton. The working order does not matter, but you may find it best to work the areas of satin stitch first (some of the main parts of the design).

Finishing off
When all the stitching is complete, check that the back of the work is neat, and remove it from the frame. Press it gently on the wrong side using a damp cloth and a warm iron. Before having the work framed – or framing it yourself – mount it on a piece of fairly thick white board (from art shops). Cut the board to the required size. Remember to allow for the frame overlap (usually 6mm/¼in). Trim fabric to 4cm/1½in larger all round than the board. Place work face down on a clean surface with the board centrally on top. Bit by bit, stretch fabric over the board, pinning it along the cut edge of the board and lacing opposite sides together across the back with a needle and strong thread. Tuck surplus fabric neatly under at the corners.

25

Trace pattern and stitch guide

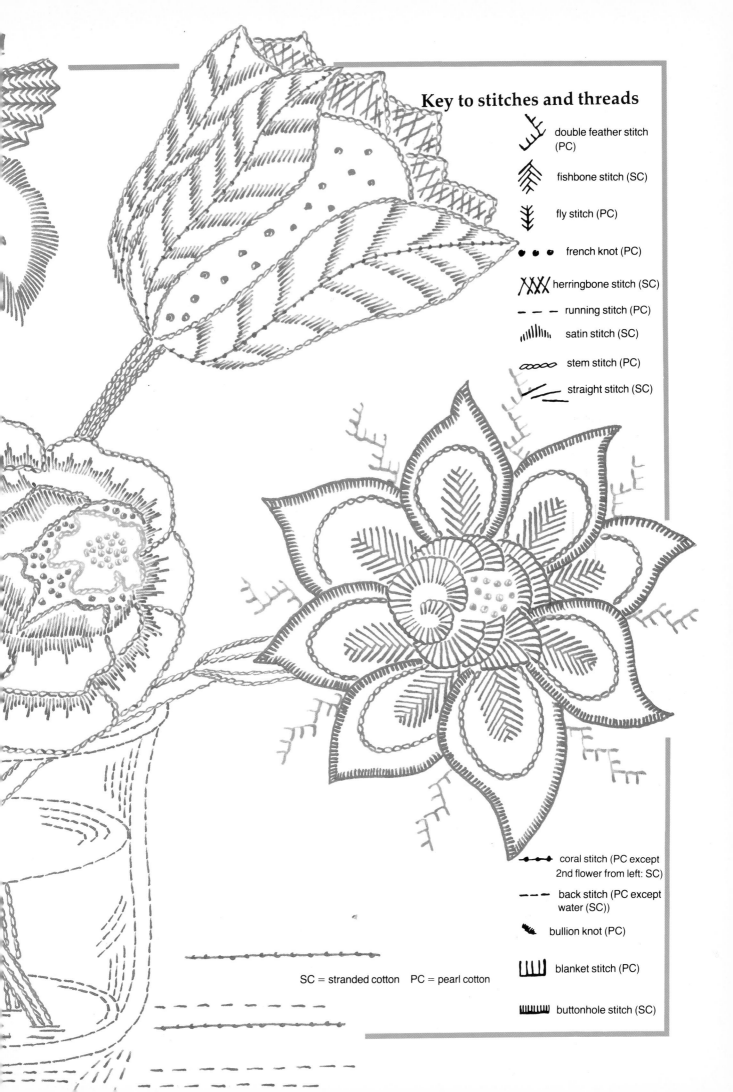

Key to stitches and threads

double feather stitch (PC)

fishbone stitch (SC)

fly stitch (PC)

• • • french knot (PC)

XXX herringbone stitch (SC)

– – – running stitch (PC)

satin stitch (SC)

stem stitch (PC)

straight stitch (SC)

coral stitch (PC except 2nd flower from left: SC)

– – – back stitch (PC except water (SC))

bullion knot (PC)

blanket stitch (PC)

SC = stranded cotton   PC = pearl cotton

buttonhole stitch (SC)

Two knotted stitches

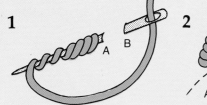

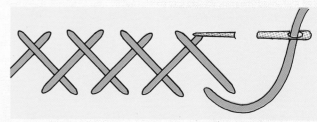

Bullion knots

1 Bring the needle up at A. Take a fairly large stitch from B to A but do not pull the needle through. Twist the thread six or seven times round the needle.

2 Pull the needle through, easing the twisted thread close to the fabric with your thumb. Re-insert the needle at B.

Coral stitch

Bring the thread through to the front of the fabric. Working from right to left, lay the thread along the stitching line, securing with your thumb. Now make a tiny stitch across the stitching line, a little distance away, under the laid-down thread and over the loop of thread to catch it in a knot. Continue making stitches an equal distance apart. Make them close together or spaced out, as you wish.

Two flat stitches

Fishbone stitch

Use this stitch to fill a shape with a central 'vein'.

1 Make a small stitch at the end of the shape, along the central vein. Bring the thread out to the right of the stitch on the outline of the shape, at A. Make a diagonal stitch, across the base of the first stitch. Bring the needle up at B, on the outline of the shape, to the left.

2 Make another stitch across the base of the last one, and continue in this way until the shape is filled.

Herringbone stitch

This is often worked between parallel lines, but may be used to fill a shape, as in the sampler. Bring the thread up on the bottom line and make a small running stitch along the opposite line, so that the thread lies diagonally across the fabric. Note that the stitch is worked from left to right, but the needle always points from right to left. Now make a small running stitch to the right of the first one, and along the bottom line. Continue, leaving a small space between running stitches.

Two looped stitches

Feather stitch

Bring the thread through to the front of the fabric. Make a loose stitch by inserting the needle level with this point, and bring it up lower down, so that when the thread is looped under the needle, it makes a V. Pull the needle through. Make stitches to right and left alternately.

Double feather stitch

Make three stitches to the right, then make two to the left, two to the right, and so on. Slope the needle from right to left when working to the right, and vice versa.

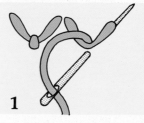 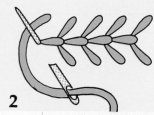

Fly stitch

Work this stitch singly, or in vertical rows.

1 Make a V-shaped stitch as for feather stitch, and make a running stitch to hold the V in place. This may be as long or as short as you wish and finishes a single fly stitch.

2 A continuous line is made by bringing the needle up to the left of the holding stitch and making the next V at its base as shown. Work the stitches close together, or space them by lengthening the holding stitch.

CHAPTER 6

Freestyle embroidery pictures

You don't need an extensive knowledge of embroidery stitches to create a beautiful piece. The direction of the stitches and the threads used to work them play just as important a part in the overall design. Use them to convey the look of natural things, near and far.

All the embroidery shown here is worked in a surprisingly simple range of stitches – in fact most of it is created using straight stitches – worked together, separately, horizontally, vertically, slanting, long, short – in every case, the effect comes from the way in which the embroiderer has chosen to work the stitches. Careful colour choice is also an essential.

The examples below show middle distance and landscape scenes.

Middle distance tree trunks

This beautiful study shows tree trunks worked in straight stitches using a single thread of stranded cotton. Mixed tones of subtle grey and green suggest moss or lichen on the trunks, and the stitches are worked in slightly varying diagonal lines to give a feeling of form.

In contrast, the sky is entirely in horizontal stitches and shaded with two blues and white to give a delicate 'wash' effect.

A beach landscape

There are only two stitches used to create this peaceful beach scene. A small amount of fly stitch in green (page 28) picks out the vegetation at the top of the beach. All the other effects are created with straight stitches – horizontal ones for the sea, a speckled effect (use seeding, page 48) in the middle ground, and blocks of short upright stitches amongst the fly stitches. The foreground pebbles are mottled with different shades of a medium silk thread. To give a three-dimensional effect some of them are raised from the fabric with small pieces of pelmet Vilene tacked to the ground fabric. The straight stitches are worked so that they lie close together over the top.

Below: Create a picture to be proud of with nature's own colours and carefully placed straight stitches. Keep the frames simple and in neutral tones.

Dandelion days panel picture

The design for this beautiful panel is based on the life-cycle of a dandelion. This humble flower, generally regarded as a weed, is full of interest from the moment of budding to the time when the last seedhead blows away. The finished panel is divided into six sections showing the flower at different stages from bud to seedhead. An exciting range of materials has been used, to portray the flowers as realistically as possible.

You will need
0.50m/½yd lightweight unbleached calico, or natural silk noil
1 skein each Coats stranded cotton in 0269 (dark green), 0266 (mid-green), 0264 (light green), 0307 (ochre) and 0300 (cream)
1 skein Danish flower thread in 123 (bright yellow)
10 artificial flower stamens (optional)
1m/1⅛yd each narrow – 3mm/⅛in – satin ribbon in yellow and mid-green
Oddment of parcel string
12cm/5in square white felt
Crewel needles sizes 7-9
Tacking thread
Tracing or greaseproof paper
Dressmaker's carbon paper
Rectangular embroidery frame
Green and white mounting card, craft knife and steel ruler

Preparing to work the design
Cut the fabric to a rectangle at least 45cm×36cm/18in×14in. Press to remove creases and lay on a flat surface.
Trace the design from the pattern on pages 32–33 and transfer to the fabric using the dressmaker's carbon paper (see page 10).
Mount the fabric on a frame as described on page 24, making sure it is drum-tight.

Working the embroidery
Refer to the Stitch and Colour Key on pages 32–33 throughout the embroidery.
First work all the thin, stitched grasses using long stem stitches. Make the lines flowing and graceful. (Note that thicker stems are worked with two strands.)
Next, apply the ribbon grasses – cut the ribbon to the required lengths following the trace pattern. Take care to keep them smooth and flat and anchor them on each side with tiny stitches at about 5mm/¼in intervals, using a single strand of mid-green thread.

Below: The finished picture measures 30cm×37cm/12in×14½in but if you do not wish to undertake the whole piece of work, stitch a single dandelion head - in full flower or at the seed stage – to make a charming picture.

Padding and stitching the flower centres

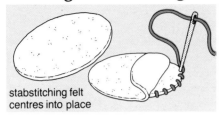

stabstitching felt centres into place

Every dandelion head is padded with felt. Using the trace pattern, cut a piece of white felt to the shape required for each.

For panels 3, 4, 5 and 6, cut out two more pieces, each slightly smaller than the previous one. Sew the smallest in position first, using tiny stab stitches. Apply the second shape over the top in the same way, then the largest over the previous two. Always bring the needle up through the background fabric and down through the felt. This prevents it from tearing.

Now, following the key, cover the shapes in panels 1, 3, 4, 5 and 6 with closely-worked satin stitch. Stitch the tiny green sepals (Panels 1, 3 and 6) in slanting satin stitch, using two strands of thread. Shorten the stitches towards the tip.

Wrapping and couching the stems

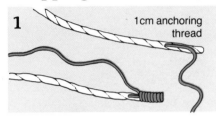

1   1cm anchoring thread

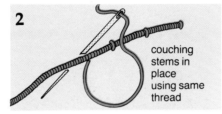

2   couching stems in place using same thread

To work the raised stems for the dandelions in panels 1, 2 and 3, cut lengths of parcel string for the cores following the trace pattern.
1 Cut three strands of mid-green thread, six times the length of the cut string. Begin wrapping from the top, first laying about 1cm/½in of thread along the string which you then cover to anchor it.

Wrap the string closely until the whole length is covered, making sure none of the core shows through. Fasten off the stranded cotton by threading it a short way back through the wrapping.
2 Now using the same thread, couch the prepared stems in position, keeping stitches 5mm/¼in apart. In panels 4, 5 and 6, work the dandelion stems in slanting straight stitches.

Petals and clocks

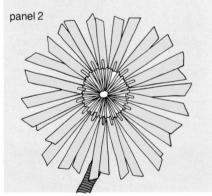

panel 2

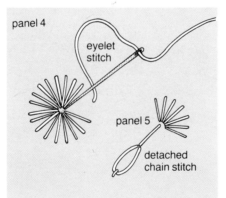

panel 4

eyelet stitch

panel 5

detached chain stitch

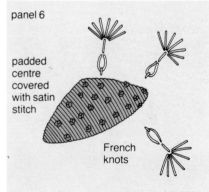

panel 6

padded centre covered with satin stitch

French knots

To work the petals in panels 1 and 3, use varying lengths of straight stitches and the Danish flower thread. Mix in a few artificial stamens (if available) at panel 1 and a little cream thread at panel 3.

In panel 2, cover the felt centre with yellow straight stitches, radiating out from the centre. Cut 15 lengths of yellow ribbon, 2.5cm/1in to 3.5cm/1½in long. Fold them in half roughly and stitch them in place around the centre with the shorter ones at the top, leaving the ends free. Use the Danish flower thread to work more straight stitches over the base of the ribbon loops and interspersed with the petals.

Panel 4 Round each padded flower head, work eyelets formed of many stitches radiating in to a centre point. Overlap them and let the stitches form the outside of the shape. Try to give a feeling of delicacy and transparency to the 'clock'.

Panel 5 Work three quarters of the 'clock' in eyelet stitch as before. Stitch three or four detached seeds flying off at different angles, with a straight stitch and a detached chain stitch under each.

Panel 6 Scatter French knots over the padded centre and add three or four seedheads blowing away.

Finishing off

Remove the fabric from the frame. Stretch the embroidery over the white mounting card, lacing it firmly across the back.

Draw out the rectangular windows on the green mounting card using the dimensions on the trace pattern. Use a sharp craft knife to cut them out. Position the card over the finished embroidery and frame – a perspex box frame is particularly suitable.

Trace pattern, stitch guide and colour key

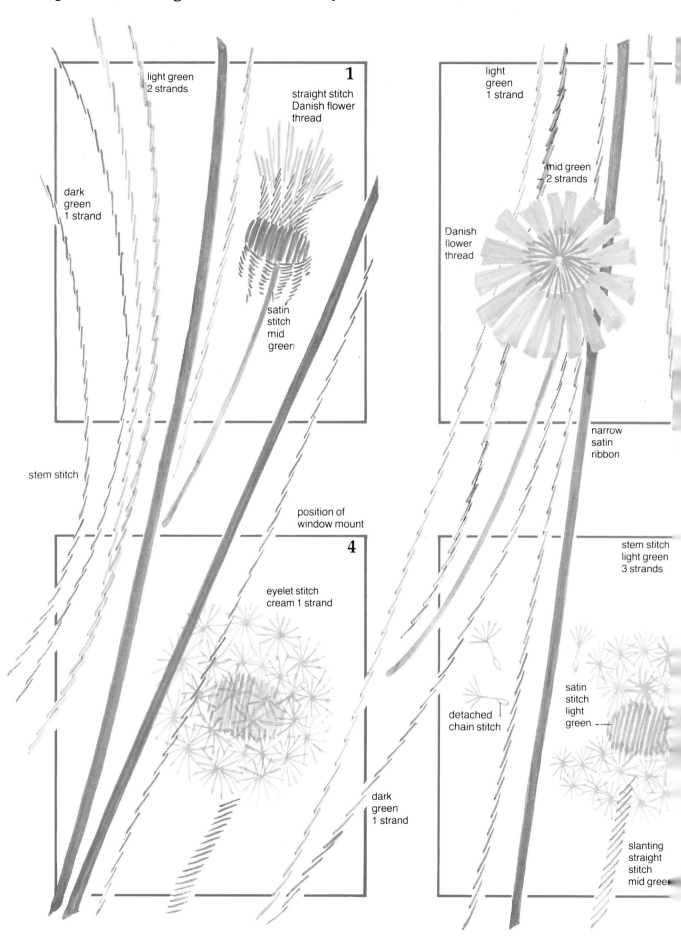

light green
2 strands

1

straight stitch
Danish flower
thread

dark
green
1 strand

light
green
1 strand

mid green
2 strands

Danish
flower
thread

satin
stitch
mid
green

stem stitch

narrow
satin
ribbon

position of
window mount

stem stitch
light green
3 strands

4

eyelet stitch
cream 1 strand

detached
chain stitch

satin
stitch
light
green

dark
green
1 strand

slanting
straight
stitch
mid green

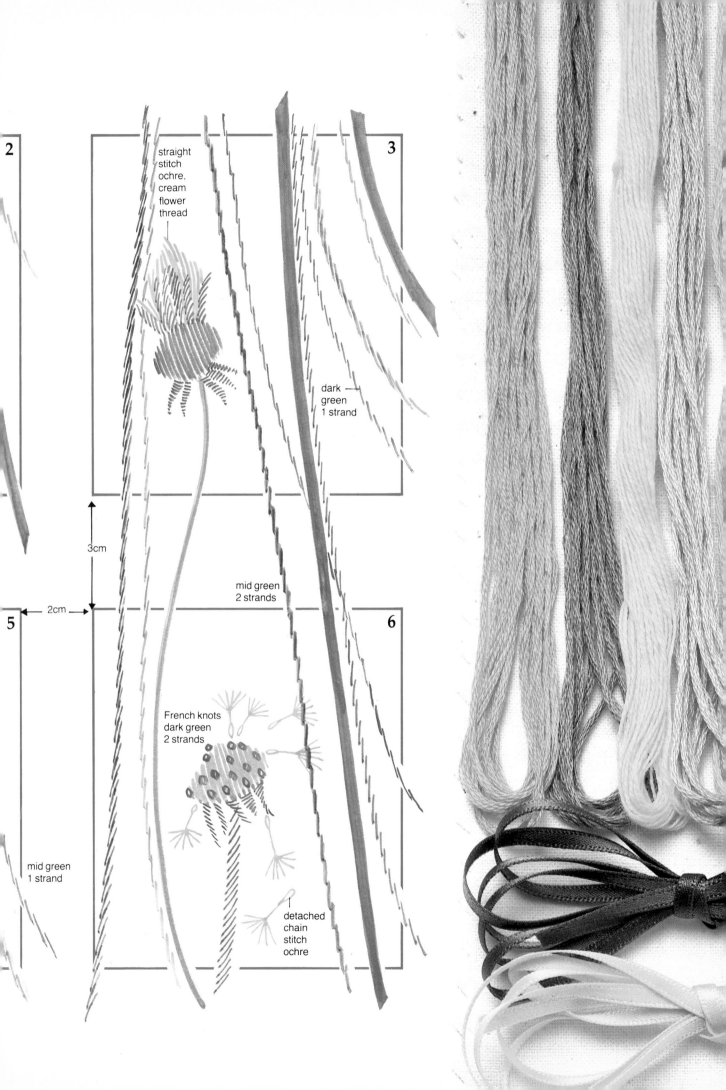

2

3

straight
stitch
ochre,
cream
flower
thread

dark
green
1 strand

3cm

2cm

mid green
2 strands

5

6

French knots
dark green
2 strands

mid green
1 strand

detached
chain
stitch
ochre

CHAPTER 7

Long and short stitches for a shaded effect

Long and short stitch, a close relation of satin stitch, allows you to create a silky, lustrous effect, as well as delicate colour-shading. It is ideal for this beautiful Chinese-style stitchery depicting glowing leaves and flowers typical of the far East.

As the name suggests, long and short stitch is worked with alternately long and short stitches. These interlock with the rows above and below, forming an all-over texture suitable for filling in motifs of all sizes and irregular shapes, particularly those too large to be filled by a row of ordinary satin stitch.

The beautiful 'painted' effect is achieved by using several different tones of one colour thread. The stitch is often used in crewel work, which is described in chapter 10, page 47.

Padded satin stitch gives a lovely plump, glossy look to simple shapes – making it a good stitch for initials. By slanting the stitches on each motif in a different direction, you can make the same shades of thread look paler or darker.

Overcasting stitch is invaluable for working flower stems or raised, curved lines.

Long and short stitch

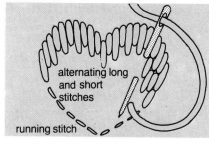

To work neatly, outline the motif to be stitched with running stitch. Work the first row, carefully following the outline of the shape with alternate long and short stitches lying very close together, as shown.

Work the next row of long stitches following the outline created by the first row. Place the stitches so that they butt up against those above, or even work slightly into the base of them. When you reach the lower edge of the motif, fill the last row with alternate long and short stitches as on the first.

Framing light fabrics

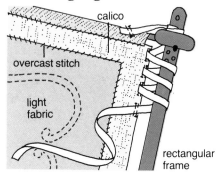

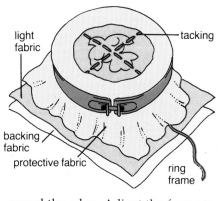

Fine embroidery deserves fine fabrics. When working embroidery on a light, flimsy fabric such as silk, it is best to back it with a firmer fabric such as calico or holland.

When using a rectangular frame Cut the calico larger than the main fabric and attach to the embroidery frame rollers.

Using cotton tape instead of twine, lash the side edges of the calico to the side stretchers, securing each loop of tape to the calico with two pins set in opposite directions, as shown. At this stage the calico should be slightly slack.

Centre the main fabric (marked with the design) on the calico, matching the grain. Pin along each edge from the centre outwards, stretching the fabric as you go, then overcast it all round the edge. Adjust the frame to make the fabric drum-tight. You can either cut away the calico backing fabric behind the main fabric before working the embroidery, or work through both layers to give extra body.

When using a ring frame Lay the main fabric over the backing fabric and tack together securely with two lines of tacking crossing at the centre. Bind the inner ring of the frame with cotton tape, then mount the two fabrics in the frame.

If the top fabric is liable to be marked by the ring (as in the case of silk, for instance), lay a third piece of spare, clean fabric over it before positioning the outer ring. Cut the protective fabric away over the area you wish to embroider.

Chinese-style bag

This exquisite little bag could well become a family heirloom. The range of colours used is astonishing – palest salmon pink shades to deep red for the flower petals, subtle shades of green for the leaves and touches of deep violet for contrast.

Work the embroidery before cutting out and making up the bag. It would look equally beautiful worked on ivory or cream silk.

If you only want to work a small amount of embroidery, trace off a part of the design – a single flower for instance – and bring a touch of oriental charm to a silk T-shirt, kimono or cushion cover.

You will need

1 skein each Twilleys Lystra stranded cotton in 532, 621, 530, 524, 724, 519, 520, 843, 544, 612, 628, 527
Crewel needles size 8
50cm/½yd black fabric – Honan silk, Antung, taffeta or other matt black silk or cotton fabric (any width)
40cm/½yd backing fabric – calico or firm cotton (any width)
Ring frame or rectangular frame
Snap fastener
2 sheets tracing or greaseproof paper

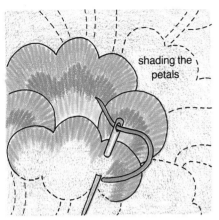

shading the petals

Overcast stitch

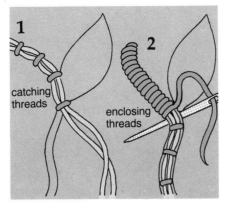

1 catching threads

2 enclosing threads

Padded satin stitch

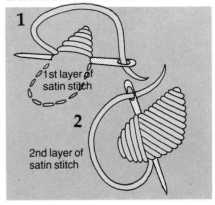

1 1st layer of satin stitch

2 2nd layer of satin stitch

Shading technique When you wish to shade gradually, such as on petals, leaves etc, change the colour of the thread. The progressively paler (or darker) tones will overlap, shading into one another.
Begin at the top of the motif and work downwards, stitching the lower petals and leaves first.
Be sure to keep all the stitches running in the same direction on each petal.

Sometimes called trailing, this is an effective way of giving stems in floral motifs an attractive, raised look.
1 Lay down a few threads on the fabric surface, along the stitching line, catching them at intervals with tiny stitches to hold the shape of the design.
2 Work neat, close, overcasting satin stitches over the top of the laid threads, to completely enclose them.

To give satin stitch more relief and add emphasis to parts of a design, work them in padded satin stitch.
1 Outline the motif in tiny chain or running stitches.
Work over the top in satin stitch, with each stitch running in the same direction, to enclose the outline.
2 Now work another layer of satin stitch over the top, running in the opposite direction to the first.

Black machine twist – same composition as main fabric
Purchased black tassel trim

Preparing the fabric
From the main fabric, cut two 30cm/ 11¾in squares and two straight crosswise strips, each 5.5cm/2¼in wide and 87cm/34in long.
Trace off the design on to tracing or greaseproof paper. Centre the tracing over one of the squares of main fabric and pin in position. Mount the fabric (and backing fabric) on whatever frame you are using, as described on the previous page. If using a rectangular frame, cut the backing fabric to 40cm/16in square. For a ring frame, cut both pieces of fabric to the same size. Stitch along the main design outlines in small running stitches through the tracing paper, using two strands of the appropriately coloured stranded cotton. This marks the design and also helps to hold the main and backing fabrics firmly together. Carefully tear away the tracing or greaseproof paper.

Right: The unusual shape of this pretty embroidered bag makes it extra special.

Working the design

Use three strands of stranded cotton throughout. Work all the petals and leaves in long and short stitch. You will find it easier to work the outer petal and leaf edges before filling in the inner areas. The secret of success is to work methodically and keep the outlines even. Work the stems and pink design outline in overcast stitch (lay down 4-8 threads underneath, depending on thickness of lines), and the remainder of the design in padded satin stitch.

Finish off each thread neatly and snip it off at the back before beginning the next colour. This prevents you from bringing up strands of the wrong colour on the front of the work.

Trace pattern and colour guide

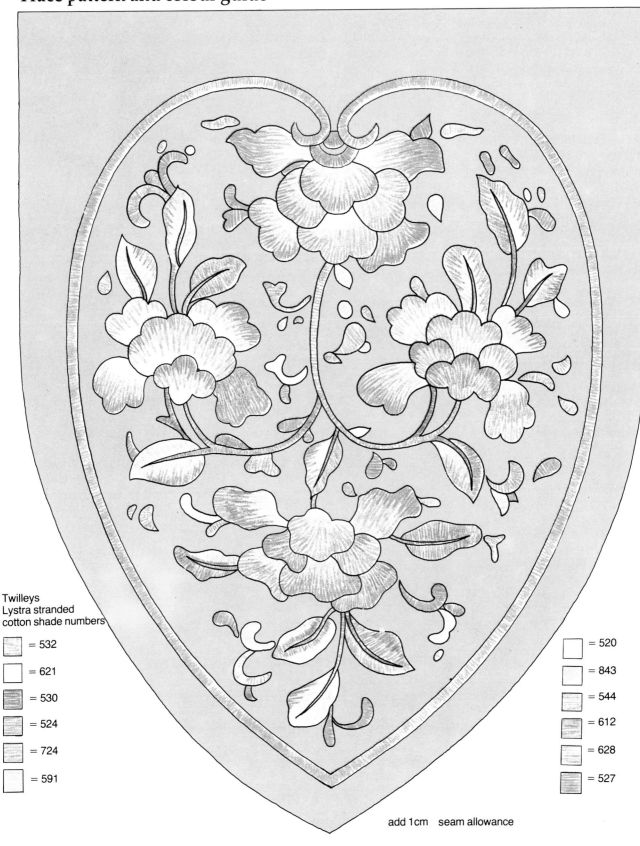

Twilleys
Lystra stranded
cotton shade numbers

☐ = 532

☐ = 621

☐ = 530

☐ = 524

☐ = 724

☐ = 591

☐ = 520

☐ = 843

☐ = 544

☐ = 612

☐ = 628

☐ = 527

add 1cm   seam allowance

Making up the bag

Remove main fabric and backing from the frame. Make a tracing paper pattern piece from the outline given and use it to cut out the bag front (embroidered) and back. When cutting out, add 1cm/½in seam allowance all round. Cut an extra piece in backing fabric for lining the back. Tack the bag back and back lining together along seamline (1cm/½in in from edges). Turn over 5mm/¼in on top edges of bag back and front; turn over a further 5mm/¼in and topstitch. Place the two long strips of fabric right sides together and join with a 1cm/½in seam. Then join the two remaining short ends with a 1cm/½in seam, to make a continuous band for the 2cm/¾in wide bag strap and gusset. Press seams open. With right sides together, and placing one strip seam at lower point of bag, pin and tack one long side strip to bag front, taking a

1cm/½in seam. Stitch, taking particular care around curves. Now pin other long side of strip to bag back, taking a 1cm/½in seam allowance on the bag side and a 2.5cm/1in seam on the strip. Stitch. On the strap, press under 5mm/¼in on deeper seam allowance; fold 1cm/½in allowance to middle on opposite side, lap over remaining 2cm/¾in allowance, tack and topstitch strap all round close to both edges. Inside bag, trim seams and overcast to prevent fraying. Attach tassel trim to bottom of bag and snap fastener at centre of top edges to close.

neatening strap

1cm

2cm

2cm

foldlines

5mm

topstitching

DESIGN EXTRA

Exotic embroidery extras for your wardrobe

You don't have to work the whole design given for the Chinese-style bag. There are many ways in which you can pick out individual motifs and use them to add a luxurious touch to special garments. Remember to work the embroidery before making up the clothes – you'll find it much easier.

Make up a simple silk T-shirt from fabric on which you have

first embroidered one of the beautiful blossoms and some of the leaves. Or position the same motif close to the front shoulder of a silky evening jacket. The centre top blossom, inverted, is a perfect motif for the front of a silk-covered cummerbund. It's not essential to stick to the colours shown here. Try working the entire design in cream and white – it would look stunning on coffee-coloured ground fabric.

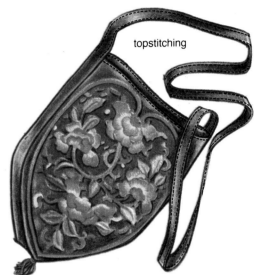

pretty motif for a party dress collar

part of bag design added to a waistcoat

coffee and cream colour scheme

decorate the flap of an evening bag

trace motif from bag design

Pattern darning for border designs

Pattern darning on evenweave fabrics allows you to create intricate patterns from simple running stitch. You can adapt all kinds of designs ranging from geometric borders for clothes and household linens to pictorial designs with varied fillings.

Darning stitches as decoration have a rich worldwide history. In Mexico and Guatemala, pattern darning decorates women's blouses with bold, geometric patterns. The blouses are

Below: Traditional pattern darned pieces show intricate geometric and stylized designs.

so covered with stitches that you have to look at the wrong side of the fabric to discover that they are not woven designs. In ancient Peru, people pattern darned geometric borders on the edges of large mantles, and the modern descendants of the Incas still decorate their ponchos with bands of these stitches. There is

also a strong European pattern darning tradition – stylized birds and flowers being popular subjects for embroidery particularly in Sweden where the technique dates back to mediaeval times and is still used today.

People in Southern Russia embroidered linen towels at either end using red silk thread. These were used to decorate the house and cover icons or ceremonial carts or sleighs. The decoration often consisted of double-headed eagles or men on horseback outlined in stem or chain stitches, filled with bands of pattern darning. The Ukraine, Greece and Northern Ethiopia also have a tradition of pattern darning.

English needlewomen this century have made pattern darning popular for decorative bands on table linen and cushions, often combining it with blackwork (see page 42).

Pattern darning techniques

By working rows of running stitch over and under the vertical or horizontal threads (warp or weft) of an evenweave fabric, you can produce patterns resembling woven brocade. Most of the thread in these patterns lies on the right side of the fabric, forming an effect of solid colour. Real woven brocade needs a more complicated loom and takes longer to weave than plain fabric, so pattern darning achieves a quicker result. The range of geometric patterns that you can create is endless. By working over different numbers of threads, try stitching zigzags, triangles, stars, crosses, squares and stripes. As with all counted threadwork, you cannot make a true curve, so figurative designs become angular and stylized.

How to work the darning

Using a tapestry needle, work in running stitch only. It is very important to count the threads accurately to achieve a neat and accurate result. Work out your pattern on graph paper first, having the grid lines representing the horizontal and vertical threads. If the pattern is complicated, lay a ruler under each row being followed. The pattern can run across the width of the fabric so that each row is worked from left to right (or right to left) and the thread finished off on each row.

Otherwise, a simple motif can be used as a scattered design all over the fabric, or can be repeated vertically to form a multi-coloured band. The darning may be all in one colour, or worked in stripes of different colours.

Take care that none of the stitches are too long as they may catch in use. It is also more difficult to keep an even tension whilst working. To darn a narrow band or a single motif, work in the hand, turning the embroidery after each row so that you are always working in the same direction. Stretch larger pieces of work in a ring or slate frame to keep an even tension. Begin with a long end of thread and weave this into the reverse side of the stitches later. Use a length of thread long enough to complete a whole motif, or to darn across the full fabric width. Fasten it off on the wrong side by weaving the end through a few of the reverse side stitches.

Right: A variety of ground fabrics including hessian, Hardanger tape, evenweave linen and Huckaback.

Types of pattern darning

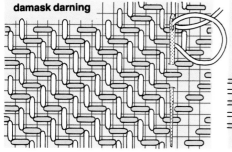

Pattern darning can take various forms according to the materials and stitches used.

Damask darning is a very striking technique which gives an effect closest to that of real damask or brocade. The darning is worked both horizontally and vertically, either in the same thread, or in two shades of one colour to give a 'shot' effect. The damask darning covers the whole surface of the fabric.

Huckaback darning is a traditional Scandinavian technique. Its characteristic appearance comes from the fact that it is worked on special Huckaback linen towelling which has regularly-spaced, long floats of threads on the right side. The embroidery needle and thread pass under these floats, diagonally as well as horizontally and vertically. Huckaback can be difficult to obtain but it is possible to work similar patterns on ordinary evenweave fabric – there will not be quite so much thread showing on the right side.

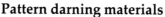

Pattern darning materials

The more loosely-woven the fabric, the easier it is to weave the needle in and out. Evenweave linen and Hardanger can be used for table linen and cushions, and even hessian and loosely woven tweed can be quite effective. For clothing projects, work the embroidery on collars, cuffs, pockets, yokes or belts.

Suitable threads depend on your choice of fabric. Stranded cotton is best for linen, Hardanger or evenweave cotton if you want a dense, smooth finish. For a lighter effect, use pearl cotton or coton à broder which will let the ground fabric show between the rows of darning. On heavier woollen fabrics, use Persian yarn or knitting yarn.

Pattern darned hand towel border

What could make a prettier present than a fluffy hand towel with an embroidered pattern across one end. There's not too much stitching to do, and a length of convenient ready-to-use Hardanger tape makes the work light and easy to handle.

Choose colours of thread to tone or form an attractive contrast with the towel. The design used here includes four different shades but you can work in as many as you like, or in the same colour throughout.

You could also use the embroidered Hardanger tape to trim a matching facecloth or sponge-bag.

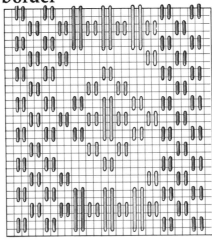

DMC stranded cotton

- 600
- 961
- 776
- 904

Chart for the motif

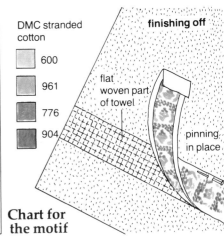

finishing off

flat woven part of towel

pinning in place

You will need

Hand towel about 40cm/16in wide
50cm/½yd of 6cm/2¼in wide white Hardanger tape (22 threads to 2.5cm/1in)
DMC stranded cotton, 1 skein each in four shades (red 600, pink 961, pale pink 776 and green 904 are used here)
Tapestry needle size 22
White sewing thread

Trimming the towel

Begin the pattern darning 2.5cm/1in away from one end of the length of tape and about 1cm/½in from top edge so the design is roughly centred.

Using the full six strands of stranded cotton and beginning with the green, follow the pattern as given on the chart working each row across the width of the tape. The horizontal and vertical lines represent the fabric threads. There is no need to finish off the thread after each colour section, just carry threads down the side of the work on the back. Repeat the pattern about 17 times (or to cover the width of the towel) – an extra six rows of green will finish off the design nicely.

Finishing off Steam press the embroidery on the wrong side. Turn under the excess tape down each long side of the work leaving 3mm/⅛in edge. Trim and turn under each end so the tape fits the towel width. Pin it in place on the flat, woven part of the towel and hem it in place.

Left: Pattern darning trims a towel – try darning a name or initials, too.

Set of pattern darned table mats and napkins

A simple pattern darned border makes a most beautiful set of table linen. These mats and napkins are of evenweave Hardanger fabric, embroidered in brightly-coloured stranded cottons. The four-way heart motif which is repeated across each mat is used singly on the corner of each napkin.

You will need

To make four table mats 41cm×30cm/16in×12in and four napkins 30cm/12in square
1m/1yd Hardanger fabric, with 150cm/60in (25 threads to 2.5cm/1in) in chosen shade
DMC stranded cotton, 2 skeins each in four shades (red 817, yellow 743, brown 433, blue 995 used here)
Tapestry needle size 22
Sewing thread to match fabric

Working the mats and napkins

From the Hardanger fabric, cut out four mats 34cm×45cm/13½in×17½in and four napkins 34cm/13½in square. This allows for turnings of 2cm/¾in.
To begin the pattern darning on a mat, place the first motif 7cm/2¾in down from the top and 2cm/¾in from the left-hand side. Follow the motif pattern given on the chart,

and using the full six strands of embroidery thread, work the motifs in the colour sequence you have chosen. Cut a 75cm/30in length of thread for each motif.
Follow the pattern for each row with a ruler to help yourself work accurately. If you find the work difficult to see, use a magnifier which hangs around the neck.
On each napkin, embroider a single motif (one in each colour), placing it 6cm/2¼in from two adjoining edges. Steam press the embroidery on the wrong side and turn in a 2cm/¾in double hem all round each mat and napkin, mitring the corners neatly. Pin, tack and hem in place. Press thoroughly.

Above: Bright, homely table settings.

Chart for motif

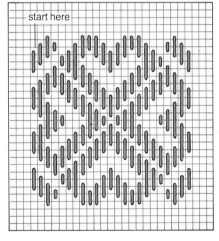

CHAPTER 9

Blackwork: block designs in geometric patterns

These intricate-looking geometric patterns are derived from Moorish designs but are worked using simple straight stitches on an evenweave fabric. Try the technique using gingham to help keep the patterns even and embroider a bright kitchen set.

Blackwork is a counted thread technique and was originally used to make beautifully embroidered clothes. Black stitches were worked on white linen and sometimes a little gold thread was included for added richness. The little geometric motifs, worked as all-over patterns, give varying densities according to the thickness of the thread and the pattern being worked.

The other traditional role for blackwork was as fillings for pictorial motifs. Designs of fruit, leaves, flow-

ers and animals, outlined in back-stitch or Holbein stitch, were filled in with different patterns forming areas of solid texture.

Blackwork is normally worked on an evenweave fabric in stranded or pearl cotton using a tapestry needle. It is not essential to stick to black and white – other colour combinations can look just as striking.

Blackwork patterns

The simplest use of blackwork is in block patterns to decorate table linen or cushions as shown opposite and page 44. Blackwork can also be used for pictorial designs but more care is needed in the choice and placing of these patterns.

Many blackwork patterns look far more complicated than they actually are. Most are built up using back-stitch or Holbein stitch combined with other straight stitches. It is the way the stitches are arranged that makes the pattern easy or compli-cated but the range of patterns is limitless and it is easy to make up your own. Samplers of different blackwork patterns can look attrac-tive and if you make your own it can be used for future reference.

Basic blackwork stitches

Small, straight stitches make up the majority of blackwork patterns. Backstitch is useful for outlining and chain stitch, coral stitch and stem stitch are occasionally used (see pages 8 and 28). Two new stitches are Holbein stitch and double cross stitch given below.

Two new stitches for blackwork

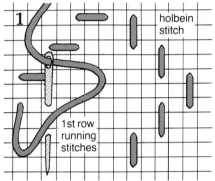

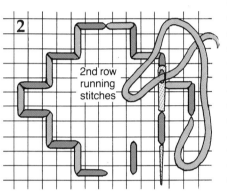

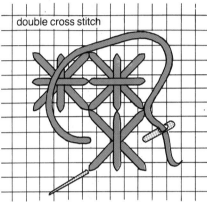

Holbein stitch

This is sometimes known as double running stitch because it combines two rows of running stitches.

1 Work a row of running stitches – passing the needle over and under the required number of threads – following the outline of your pattern.

2 Working in the opposite direction, a second row of running stitches fills in the gaps left by the first row. Try to bring the needle up very slightly to one side of the last stitch and go down slightly to the other side, for neatness.

Double cross stitch

This forms a series of star-like motifs on the fabric. First work a regular cross stitch, then work an upright cross stitch over the top with the horizontal crossing thread as the final part of the stitch. Make sure you work the stitches in the same order for each star.

Gingham kitchen set with blackwork embroidery

This set consisting of tablecloth, cushion and potholder is unusual in using gingham as a background fabric for blackwork. The stitches are placed using the checks as a guide instead of the more usual evenweave fabric and the brown and white col-our scheme adds originality to the contemporary use of this traditional technique. Use the stitch pattern guide overleaf to help you form the stitches and work from the pattern block charts which follow. The arrangement of the light, medium and dark pattern blocks gives a patchwork effect. The brown and

Left: This tablecloth is simple to embroider. Choose coloured gingham and matching thread or pick the traditional black stitching on a white background.

white gingham has square checks but it will not matter if you use a fabric with slightly rectangular checks as is the case with many ginghams.

Tablecloth

This cloth can be made for any shape of table – square, round or rectangu-lar. Measure the table first to deter-mine how much fabric you need. For a rectangular cloth such as the one shown here, follow the positioning guide overleaf for the placing of the pattern blocks. For square and round cloths, work 13 pattern blocks as given overleaf for the cushion.

You will need

For a rectangular cloth with 23 pattern blocks
Enough gingham to cover the table and give a good drop at the sides (you may have to join two widths)
8 skeins stranded cotton to match
Bias binding for edging (optional)

Working the embroidery

Find the centre of the piece of gingham by folding in quarters. In the centre check of the fabric, work the centre motif of pattern block five. (If the cloth is square or round, work the centre motif of pattern block seven.)

Keeping a row of checks between each block, work the various pattern blocks following the positioning guide, progressing outwards from the centre.

Neaten the four edges by binding with the toning bias binding, or with a double hem if you prefer.

Cushion

If your gingham has square checks the unstitched border all round the embroidery will be the same number of checks deep. If the checks are rectangular, make sure you trim the finished work so that it is square and will fit the cushion pad when seamed and bound.

You can back the cushion in a plain matching fabric as shown here but it would be more economical to use gingham as given below.

You will need

for a 50cm/20in square cushion
5 skeins stranded cotton
6mm/¼in-check gingham in chosen shade – 60cm/⅝yd of width 112cm/44in or 1.20m/1¼yd of width 90cm/36in
1 pack matching bias binding

Left: These patterns are extremely adaptable – here they are used to smarten up a gingham cushion cover.

Crewel needle, size 6
Cushion pad, 50cm/20in square
15cm/6in diameter ring frame (optional)

Working the embroidery

Cut the piece of gingham in half – lengthwise for the wider fabric, widthwise for the narrower – and set aside one of the pieces for the cushion back.

Find the centre white check of the cushion front by folding the fabric in quarters and pressing. If you have one, mount the fabric in a ring frame with this check in the centre. Begin by working a French knot in the middle of the central check, using the full six strands of stranded cotton.

Complete the rest of pattern block 7, placing knots in the white squares only. Leave a row of checks all round the block before working the next block diagonally from the first and continue adding pattern

Stitch pattern guide

Each pattern is worked on an area of 13 checks by 13 checks. The stitch patterns show up well because they are worked mainly in the white checks.

For a slightly lighter effect, use only three or four strands of the embroidery thread. Remember not to pull the needle too tightly.

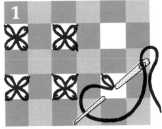

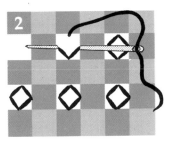

1 Work four detached chain stitches in the white checks only. The stitches are caught down at the four corners.

2 Using backstitch, make a diamond in each of the white checks in the block as shown.

3 Work a double cross stitch in each of the white checks.

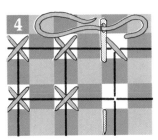

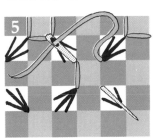

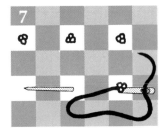

4 Work Holbein stitch between the centres of each white check until you have stitched a framework over the whole block. Now work a regular cross stitch in each white check, covering the ends of the Holbein stitches.

5 Stitch a bird's foot motif in each white check using straight stitches. Each bird's foot has three stitches, all beginning in one corner of the check and running to the opposite corner, and the centres of the two opposite sides. Follow the pattern chart to see

the angle of each bird's foot.
Now outline every other central dark check with a backstitch square, again following the chart.
6 Work a cross stitch in each white check. Now run a thread in and out between each vertical line of crosses without

piercing the fabric as shown, starting at the bottom right of the edge cross stitch. Run a second thread down the other side of the row starting bottom left of first stitch.
7 Work a French knot in the centre of each white check.

blocks until you have a chequerboard effect of alternately embroidered and free blocks. Do not pull any of the stitches up so tightly that the fabric puckers.

Making up the cushion

When all the pattern blocks have been stitched, trim the sides of the fabric outside the embroidery to make a 50cm/20in square making sure the pattern is placed centrally. With right sides together stitch bias binding round the edge of the cushion front. Place the fold of the binding on the line between the first and second rows of checks and sew along this line.

Cut the cushion back to the same size as the front and stitch front to back, wrong sides together. Leave a 28cm/11in gap along one side for inserting the cushion pad. Insert the pad, fold the bias binding to the back and hem in place over seam, closing opening at the same time.

Matching potholder

Make one or two of these quick and easy potholders and work embroidery on both sides. Double the fabric and wadding requirements for two potholders.

You will need

For one 22cm/8¾in square potholder
25cm/¼yd of 6mm/¼in square gingham
1 skein stranded cotton
1 pack matching bias binding
25cm/¼yd cotton wadding

Working the embroidery

Cut two 22cm/8¾in gingham squares. Embroider two blackwork pattern blocks on each fabric square, making sure that the corners where the blocks meet are at the centre of the square. Choose whichever patterns you like – up to four different ones.
Cut four 22cm/8¾in squares of wadding and stitch a double layer to the back of each square. Add bias binding and join the squares in the same way as for the cushion but without an opening. Make a hanging loop from binding and sew to one corner.

Below: A quickly embroidered potholder makes an ideal small present.

Pattern block charts for blackwork

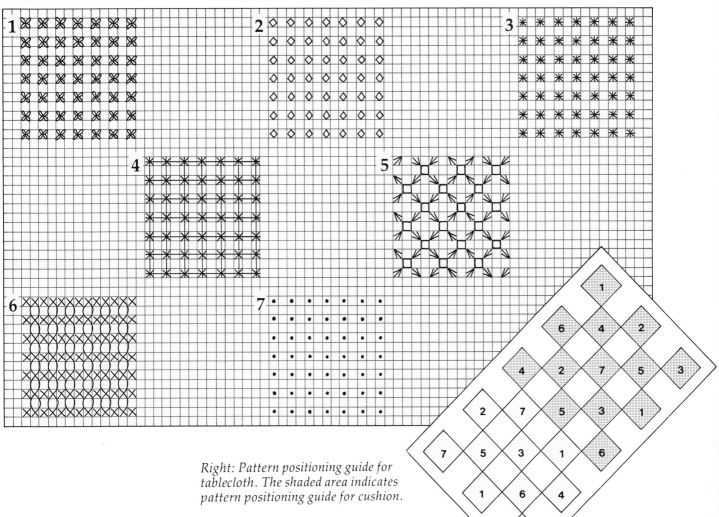

Right: Pattern positioning guide for tablecloth. The shaded area indicates pattern positioning guide for cushion.

45

Trace pattern for embroidery

Here is a pretty motif which would be ideal for crewel embroidery. Use it for a picture or a cushion cover. Transfer it onto your fabric and work with crewel wools or stranded cotton, either in outline stitches or by filling in the shapes.

CHAPTER 10

Traditional crewel work

Crewel embroidery is traditionally English, inspired by designs on 17th and 18th century Indian chintzes.
Its rich colours and shaded effects make it ideal for this lovely cushion – learn some typical crewel stitches and use some old favourites too.

Crewel designs are usually flowing abstract floral patterns, sometimes with birds, animals and trees included.

Like many traditional crewel designs, this one is worked in wool – a twisted Persian yarn – with stranded cotton used for smaller details. See design on pages 50–51.

Stitch techniques show a combination of filling and outlining with some couching (laid work). All the new stitches you need are shown on pages 48–49. Given in earlier chapters are long and short stitch and padded satin stitch (pages 34 and 35), chain stitch, backstitch and straight stitch (page 8), French knots (page 17), fly stitch and coral stitch (page 28).

Cover design lines with your stitches, carefully following motif contours and directions with stitches such as long and short and fly stitch.

Below: Pick out separate motifs from the cushion design to use individually.

Trellis stitches

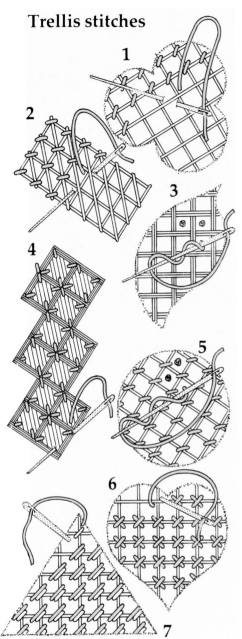

Stitches you will need

These attractive stitches are characteristic of crewel patterns. It is essential to work on a frame.

Trellis stitches

Trellis 1 Begin by laying evenly spaced threads across the area to be filled with all threads parallel. Next lay a second group of threads, across the first ones, forming squares. These long stitches only show on the reverse of the fabric. Tie each intersection of the crossing threads with a small couching stitch as shown. These stitches are often worked in a contrasting colour.

Trellis 2 Work as for trellis 1, but before couching the threads, add a third set, laid diagonally.

Trellis 3 Lay a set of double threads vertically, then weave two threads across them, close together and finish with a French knot in the centre of each square.

Trellis 4 Lay a set of double parallel threads, then lay another set across them, making exact squares between them.
Fill these squares with satin stitch as shown and finish with four tiny straight stitches at each intersection of laid threads. These stitches do not quite meet.

Trellis 5 Work as for trellis 1, adding a French knot in each square.

Trellis 6 Work as for trellis 1, but tie intersections with cross stitch.

Trellis 7 Work as for trellis 1, working two straight stitches at intersections, one slightly longer than the other.

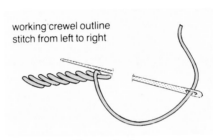

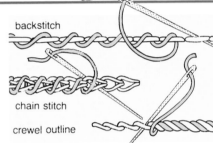

Crewel outline stitch

This stitch is widely used in crewel designs, both as an outline or, in several rows, as a filling. It is very similar to stem stitch.
Work from left to right with the thread towards you, bringing the needle up along the design line each time, at the end of the previous stitch.

Whipped stitches

Whipping is the technique of emphasizing a line stitch by threading it with a new length of yarn, sometimes in a new shade. Use a tapestry needle and pass it once through each stitch along the line, in the same direction each time, to give a raised, corded effect. Do not catch any of the ground fabric.

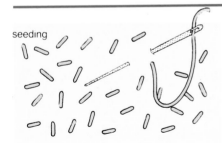

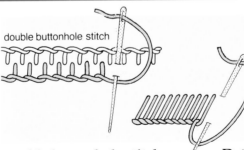

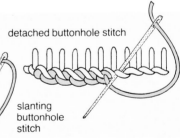

Seeding

Make a series of tiny backstitches to fill an open area, placing them an even distance apart and at different angles, scattered over the fabric.

Double buttonhole stitch

Work two interlocking rows of buttonhole stitch, as shown.
Slanting buttonhole stitch A row of regular buttonhole stitches, close together, with the long parts sloping sideways in the direction you are working.

Detached buttonhole stitch

Add an extra row of stitching to the looped edge of buttonhole stitch to make a raised frill. Using a tapestry needle, work one stitch into each loop, being careful not to catch the fabric. Do not pull stitches too tightly.

48

Twisted chain stitch

A chain stitch variation which produces a textured line – the stitches can twist either way. It looks most effective when the loops are worked close together.

1 After bringing the needle up and looping the thread round it, re-insert it slightly above (or below) where it came up before, bringing it up along the stitching line and

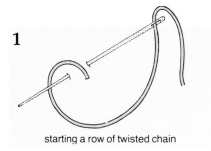

starting a row of twisted chain

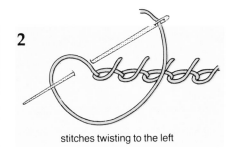

stitches twisting to the left

catching the loop.
2 Repeat for subsequent stitches,

remembering to re-insert the needle outside the loop, not inside.

A crewel embroidered cushion

To avoid confusing subtle colours, make yourself a colour guide by attaching small pieces of yarn to a card and marking the appropriate shade numbers against them.

You will need

½m/½yd ivory embroidery satin
2 crewel needles
1 tapestry needle
Paterna Persian yarn, 1 skein each in 583, 513, 269, 274, 287, 145, 492, 380, 381 and 382
2 skeins each in 573, 563, 280, 286, 462 and 466
DMC stranded cotton, 1 skein each in 3052, 932, 931, 758 and 356
Water erasable marker
½m/½yd furnishing fabric, for backing
35cm/14in zip
Piping cord (optional)
45cm/17½in cushion pad

Preparing to work the design

Enlarge the design so that 1 square equals 5cm/2in. Transfer it to the fabric using the window method (see page 10). Use one strand Persian yarn or three strands stranded cotton. Practise any new stitches first, on spare fabric. Mount the fabric in a taped ring frame (remove it when not working) or a rectangular frame, and make sure it is 'drum tight'.
Follow the working order carefully – it starts with the easier motifs and progresses to more difficult ones.

Motif A

Outer petals: lay trellis 1 (145) and tie intersections (381)
Outer edges: crewel outline (145)
Petal centres: long and short stitch (492, shading to 466 at base).
Crewel outline (274)
Leaves: outline with chain stitch

(573), line with another row (563), fill centres with crewel outline (583)

Motif B

Centre: fill with French knots (462), surrounding with slanted satin stitch (573), outer edge in twisted chain stitch (563)
Remaining space: seeding (492)

Motif C

Leaves: fly stitch (573)
Flower centres: lay trellis 1 (462) and tie intersections (145)
Flower petals: long and short stitch (shade some 287 to 286, others 286 to 280 or 280 to 274)
Centres: crewel outline (145)

Motif D

Long and short stitch, starting at turned-over tip (573 shading to 563, shade lower part similarly with 513 and 563)

Motif E

Centre petal: lay trellis 2 (280, then 274) and tie at intersections (381)
Circle: padded satin stitch (382) and crewel outline (274)
Outer petals: long and short stitch (492 shading to 466, a little 462)
Crewel outline trellis (274)
Leaves: crewel outline (573) and whip (563)
Centre vein: crewel outline (573) and whip (583)
Leaf centres: fly stitch (513)

Motif F

Lower part edges: twisted chain stitch (573 lower side, 563 upper side). Add small straight stitches inside (462 lower, 466 upper)
Flowers and stems: using stranded cotton, detached chain stitch (some 932 and some 931, with French knot centres (758 and 356)

Crewel outline their stems and work tiny detached chain stitch leaves (3052). Add two extra French knots (356) on stems (3052)
Leaf tip: slanting satin stitch (513 upper part, 563 lower)

Motif G

Three small leaves: fly stitch (563 outer two, 573 centre)
Each side of centre: three rows of whipped crewel outline (269, then 274, then 280)
Centre: padded satin stitch (466) long straight stitches lengthwise over the satin stitch (462)
Outer area: slanting satin stitch (286)
Larger leaf, beginning at the top: chain stitch (513) with French knots in centre of each chain (466). Repeat twice more, (563 with 462 knots, 573 with 145 knots)
Between these three rows, work crewel outline (466, 492, 466 between the first two, 462 between the next two, outlining lower edge with 145)
Smaller leaf: crewel outline filling (563 outer, 466, 462, 573 in centre)

Motif H

Centre part: lay trellis 3 (380 and 381 close up, French knots in 145)
Double buttonhole area round trellis (466 outer, 462 inner)
Upper part of large leaf: long and short stitch (563 shading to 573)
Upper edge: crewel outline (573 and 583)
Lower edge: crewel outline (573, whip with 583), fill with slanted satin stitch (274)
Between the long and short stitch and the satin stitch: crewel outline (583). Fit a line of crewel outline (563) below the satin stitch
Smaller leaf: fill outer section with

Graph for embroidered cushion

1 square = 5cm

slanting satin stitch (563)
Centre vein: chain stitch (462), work over with backstitch (269), crewel outline round base of satin stitch (466)

Motif I
Lower part: lay trellis 4 (573), satin stitch filling (shades 492 to 466 to 462), tie (280)
Upper part: slanted satin stitch (563)
All lines: crewel outline (573) with upper vein (583)

Motif J
Outer edge: twisted chain stitch (563) another row inside it (573)
Centre area: long and short stitch (shade from 563 outer to 573 inner)
Remaining area: French knots, widely spaced (583)

Motif K
Flower centre: trellis 5 (lay in 381), tie (380), French knots (462)
Petals: long and short stitch (shade two petals 287 to 280, two 286 to 274, and one 280 to 269)
Crewel outline round trellis (380)

Motif L
Upper side: slanting satin stitch (563)
Lower section: trellis 1 (lay in 573), tie (462)
Between satin stitch and trellis: one row crewel outline, (573) continue to form stem, one row chain stitch (145), and one row crewel outline (583), continue down stem
Below trellis: crewel outline (583), chain stitch (466), crewel outline (462) on outer lower edge

Motif M
Upper edge: chain stitch (462) with a French knot in each chain (274), next row repeat (145 with 269)
Lower edge: slanting buttonhole begin at tip (466, then 462 and repeat), knots on outside
Centre: detached chain stitch (381) with a French knot in each (462)

Motif N
Outer sections: long and short stitch (513 shading through 563 to 573)
Centre vein: chain stitch (583), whipped (462).
Rest of centre area: crewel outline (583)

Motif O
Central area: lay trellis 6 (380 and

381 close up, lay 381 and 380 across), cross stitch (462)
Petals: Long and short stitch – crewel outline overlapping petals first and work over the top (269, 274, 280, 286, a little 287)
Leaves: whipped crewel outline filling (583, 573, 563 alternating)

Motif P
Lower part: lay trellis 7 (563), tie with (563), longer stitch (466). Outline with chain stitch (573), cover this with backstitch (583) continuing to tip and fill tip with coral stitch (513 and 563), alternating knots on adjoining rows

Motif Q
Lay trellis 7 (563), tie (462), use chain stitch (573) and backstitch (145) as leaf P.
Tip: round off in slanted satin stitch (563)

Motif R
Trellis as leaves P and Q tied (145). Chain stitch and backstitch as P and Q, tip as Q

Motif S
Centre circle: padded satin stitch (492)
Inner petals: buttonhole stitch and detached buttonhole (280)
Crewel outline centre circle (466)
Middle petals: blocks of buttonhole and detached buttonhole (alternating 462, 466 and 513)
Outer petals: same as inner and middle (286 and 280).

Stems
Work all stems and remaining leaf veins in crewel outline using a combination of 583, 573 and 563.

Making up the cushion
Remove fabric from frame and trim to a 48cm/19in square. Cut backing fabric to the same size and join with right sides together, inserting zip along one edge and inserting piping if desired. Take 1.5cm/⅝in seams. Turn, and insert cushion pad.

CHAPTER 11

Mountmellick embroidery: a form of whitework

White stitchery on white fabric is a traditional choice for some of the prettiest and most prized embroideries. Here are five new stitches you'll need for the typical Mountmellick work tablecloth with its lovely raised and embossed look.

Whitework is the name generally given to white embroidery on a white background, of which one of the most distinctive types is Mountmellick work. This traditional technique from Ireland was introduced in about 1825 by a lady of the Society of Friends, Johanna Carter, to provide work for the poor people of the town of Mountmellick.

It was originally worked on white satin jean (a strong cotton fabric) with the stitchery in varying thicknesses of knitting cotton. This was used to make household articles such as bedspreads and pillow cases. A finer version for pinafores and dresses was worked on linen, sateen or cashmere, sometimes with silk thread. Designs were usually naturalistic – blackberries, passion-flowers, oak leaves, acorns, ferns and wheat being the most popular. Highly padded satin stitch was used for flowers with French knots being another distinctive feature.

Its popularity was influenced by fashion. Later revivals, in the 1880's and 1930's, added new stitches, and today any suitable surface stitch can be seen in Mountmellick work.

Right: A classic example of Mountmellick work. Most forms of whitework have open spaces, this does not. Threads and fabrics are comparatively heavy.

Useful stitches for Mountmellick embroidery

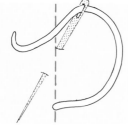

1

Portuguese knotted stem stitch
It is easiest to start this stitch by working away from you, but you can continue in any direction.
1 Make the first stem stitch in the usual way.

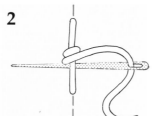

2

2 Pass the needle from right to left under this stitch, but without piercing the fabric. Repeat, making two little coils round the stitch.

3

3 Now make another regular stem stitch, along the stitching line with the needle coming up close to the two little coils.

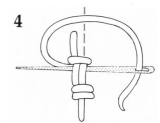

4

4 Pass the needle under both stem stitches, twice, as before.
Continue repeating steps 3 and 4.

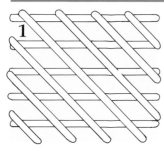

1

Honeycomb filling
1 Lay a set of threads horizontally across the space to be filled, taking care to space them evenly, then lay a set of threads diagonally across the first.

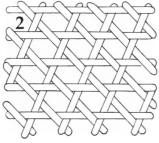

2

2 Weave a third set of threads under the horizontal and over the diagonal threads as shown, locking the pattern in place.

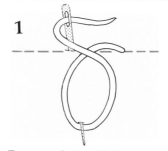

1

Rosette chain stitch
Work from right to left.
1 Bring the needle out at the start of the stitching line. Make a thread loop and take the needle through the fabric, behind the thread and through the loop. Do not pull too tightly.

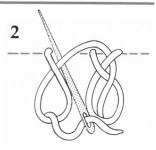

2

2 Pass the needle up and under the thread to the right of the loop. Do not pierce the fabric. You are now ready to make the next stitch.

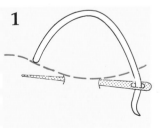

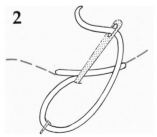

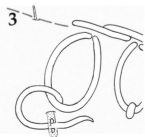

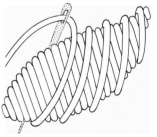

Petal stitch
This stitch creates an effect of detached chain stitches hanging from a stem stitch line. Work from right to left.
1 Bring the thread out close to the beginning of the line. Insert the needle at the beginning and

bring it out again halfway along the stitch formed.
2 Make an oblique chain stitch as shown, slanting it in the direction of the stitching line.
3 Take a stitch over the loop to secure it and bring the needle out

along the line to be stitched. Then insert the needle at the top of the chain stitch just worked. Bring it out at the end of the first stem stitch, ready to work the next chain.

Whipped satin stitch
This makes a good ribbed effect for stalks and leaves. Fill the space to be covered with regular satin stitch. Lay a set of stitches across the satin stitches, approximately at right angles and a short distance apart.

Circular tablecloth with Mountmellick embroidery

There are four identical passion flower motifs in the centre of this pretty tablecloth. Stitch the design first and make up the cloth afterwards, choosing a square or circular edge.

You will need
For a 114cm/45in cloth
Piece of medium-weight embroidery linen or similar, 122cm/48in square
12 skeins DMC Retors à broder (white)
2 skeins DMC pearl cotton No 5 (white)
Crewel needles size 6

Rectangular frame, at least 45cm/18in wide
Tracing paper and dressmaker's carbon paper
A fine, coloured pencil

Marking the design
Fold the fabric in four and mark with tacking along the straight grain of the folds. Trace off the motif outlines and the red dotted lines. Place the tracing in position on the fabric, matching tacking and dotted lines and transfer the motif using dressmaker's carbon paper. Repeat for each quarter of the design.

Framing up the design
The embroidery is quite thick and chunky, so mount the fabric on a frame if possible. If the frame is 90cm/36in or wider, mount the fabric on top and bottom rollers as usual, folding in excess fabric at the sides. Tack pieces of tape or spare fabric down the folded sides and lash these to the stretchers. With a smaller frame, mount a piece of calico on it. Stretch the embroidery fabric over this and pin and tack in place. Cut away the calico behind the part to be embroidered, then tighten up the tension on the frame.

Trace pattern for passion flower motif

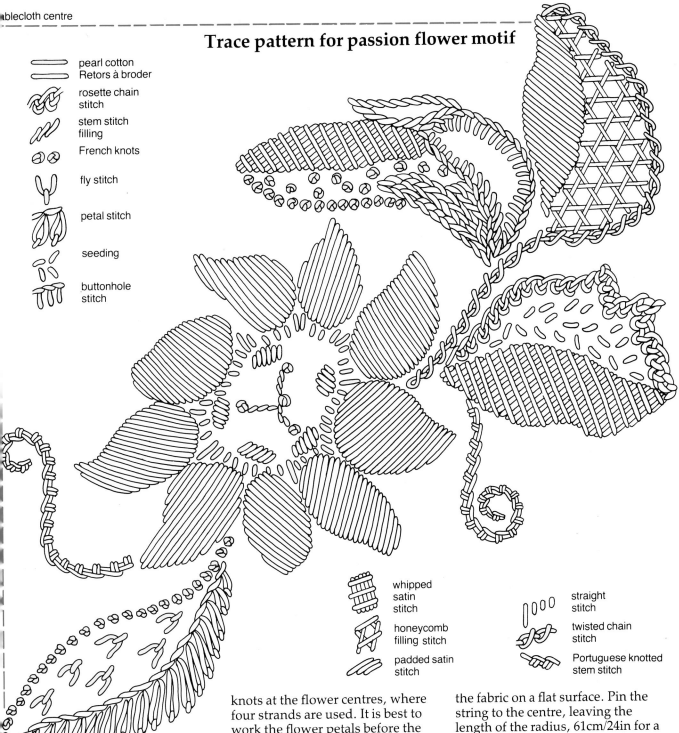

	pearl cotton
	Retors à broder
	rosette chain stitch
	stem stitch filling
	French knots
	fly stitch
	petal stitch
	seeding
	buttonhole stitch

	whipped satin stitch
	honeycomb filling stitch
	padded satin stitch

	straight stitch
	twisted chain stitch
	Portuguese knotted stem stitch

Working the embroidery

Follow the stitch key throughout, and note which parts of the design are worked in pearl cotton and which in matt cotton.

For the padded satin stitch petals (page 35), work over two layers of padding.

Use two strands of pearl cotton throughout, except for the French knots at the flower centres, where four strands are used. It is best to work the flower petals before the centres.

Where there is honeycomb filling, work this first, then outline.

Finishing off

Take the work off the frame and press lightly on the back. Any stitch marks left from framing the work can be removed by scraping gently along the weave in both directions with a finger nail.

To make a circular table cloth, use a piece of string or a tape measure with a pencil tied to the end. Lay the fabric on a flat surface. Pin the string to the centre, leaving the length of the radius, 61cm/24in for a 114cm/45in diameter cloth.

Mark out the circumference with short strokes of the pencil. Trim away excess fabric leaving an even amount all round for hem. To prevent a wavy edge, run a line of machine staystitching around marked hemline, taking care not to stretch the fabric.

Turn under the hem to staystitching, pin, tack and press. Hem by hand or machine, then remove all tacking before the final pressing.

CHAPTER 12

Cutwork motifs for a delicate openwork tracery

Cutwork embroidery is one of the prettiest ways of decorating household linens or even clothes. The design is worked in simple buttonhole stitch and then parts of the fabric are cut away from the finished embroidery to give a delicate lacy look.

There are several types of embroidery which come under the heading of openwork. One of these techniques is cutwork where the open spaces create part of the design or outline it. Cutwork edgings, where a decorative edge is worked in buttonhole stitch and the fabric cut away be-neath, add a pretty finish. Running stitch is used for outlining motifs before edging them in a close neat buttonhole stitch.

In cutwork, the stitched design is worked first and the areas of fabric to be removed are then cut away. If comparatively large areas of fabric are cut away, the open spaces are made stronger and prettier by the addition of buttonhole bars, which run between two solid areas of fabric. The stitchery is then known as Renaissance work.

Stitch the butterfly on a tablecloth or traycloth or use the alternative design as a decorative motif.

Materials Choose a firm fabric which does not fray easily, such as lawn or closely-woven linen. Stranded or pearl cotton and crewels are probably the best choice of thread and needles. You will need a small, sharp pair of pointed embroidery scissors for cutting away the fabric when the stitching is completed. For best results, work in a ring frame, although this is not essential.

Right: Pale pastels or white are the best colours for this butterfly cloth.

The technique of cutwork

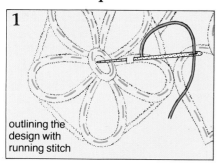

outlining the design with running stitch

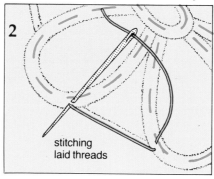

stitching laid threads

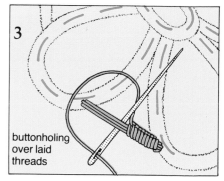

buttonholing over laid threads

Mark the design lightly on the fabric. Designs are sometimes printed with double lines. This shows the width of the buttonhole stitches to be worked along the outline.

1 Secure the thread with a backstitch and outline the design in neat running stitches about 3mm/⅛in long. Stitch between the double lines or close to the cutting edge. This helps to strengthen the cut edges of the design.

2 Buttonhole bars If the design you are working includes any buttonhole bars, stitch these next. Insert the needle at one side and take the thread across to the far side of the area to be spanned by the bar, and catch it securely into the fabric.

Bring the thread back to where it started and again catch it securely. Repeat once more so that you have three threads laid over the fabric surface.

3 The bar is worked by buttonholing over the laid threads from one end to the other without catching in any of the fabric underneath. Keep the knotted ends of the stitches in line.

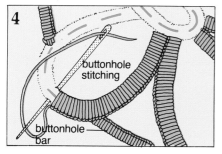

buttonhole stitching

buttonhole bar

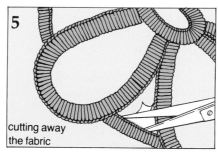

cutting away the fabric

4 When all the bars are complete, work the rest of the buttonhole stitch along the outlines of the areas to be cut out. In this way, the ends of each bar are neatly covered. Make sure that the knotted side of the buttonhole stitch lies along the side to be cut to reinforce it and give a neater finish. Anchor all threads securely, and clip off any ends. When all the embroidery is complete, take the work out of the frame if you have used one.

5 Using very sharp embroidery scissors, cut away the fabric in the appropriate areas. Cut as close as you can to the buttonhole stitches. The knots of the buttonhole should hide any fluffiness left by the ends of the fabric threads. Take care not to cut the bars as you work.

A butterfly tablecloth in Renaissance work

Once you have learnt the basics of simple cutwork, you can make this beautiful tablecloth, adorned with butterfly motifs stitched in the same colour as the fabric. The one shown here has four butterflies on it, but even just one would make a charming and delicate cloth.

Apart from the running and buttonhole stitches, chain stitch has

been used to give additional padding to the stitching and some interlaced backstitch adds a pretty touch to the head and wings.

You will need
For a cloth 115cm/45in square:
1.20m/1⅜yd cotton (heavy poplin) or linen fabric 115cm/44in wide *or* a ready-made cloth in a firmly

woven fabric
1 skein matching stranded cotton for each butterfly motif
1 skein coton à broder No 16
1 crewel needle size 8
1 tapestry needle size 24
Tracing paper and dressmaker's carbon paper
Ring frame large enough to hold the motif comfortably (optional)

Stitching the motif for cutwork

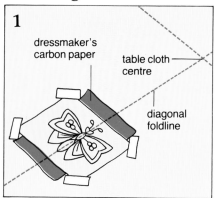

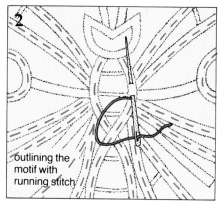

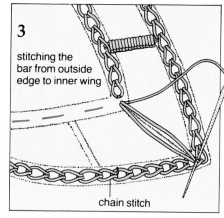

Preparing the fabric First trim the piece of fabric so that it is square. To transfer the butterflies to the fabric, trace the required number on to tracing paper and arrange them on the fabric. To make sure you place the butterfly motifs accurately at the corners of the square, fold it in two diagonally and position the body of the butterfly along one of these diagonal lines. Leave about 20cm/8in between the motif and the edge of the fabric or cloth. Secure the tracings with small pieces of adhesive tape.

1 Place the fabric on a firm, smooth surface such as a table. Slip a piece of dressmaker's carbon paper between the tracing paper and the fabric, and trace the outlines so that

a clear, but faint line is produced on the fabric.
Remove all the papers and tape and mount one motif in a ring frame, if you have one.

Outlining the motifs The areas to be cut away are shaded on the trace pattern. As this cutting will weaken the fabric, the edges to be cut must be strengthened.
Thread a crewel needle with coton à broder and, starting at the body, secure the thread with a backstitch and stitch around the outer and inner edges of each wing, outlining the shaded areas with neat running stitches about 3mm/⅛in long. The stitches should run midway between the two lines which indicate the width of final stitching.

2 Stitch round the spots on the wing in the same way and finally stitch round the body working in a figure of eight. The weakest point in the design will be strengthened where the stitches cross.
3 With coton à broder in the needle, and starting at the body, work over the running stitch with fine chain stitch, along the *outside* edges of the wings. On the inside line, work along until you reach the first bar. Secure the chain stitch by catching down the last loop and coming up again in that stitch.

Working the bars Take the thread across to the far side of the chain stitch on the outside edge and catch the thread securely in the fabric, coming up close to the inside edge

Trace pattern for butterfly

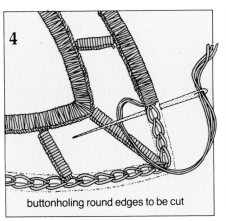

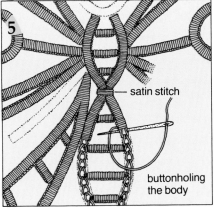

satin stitch

buttonholing the body

buttonholing round edges to be cut

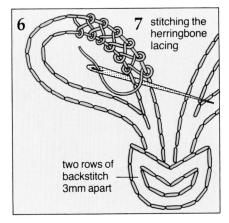

7 stitching the herringbone lacing

two rows of backstitch 3mm apart

of the chain stitch.

Bring the thread back to the side you are working, catch it securely in the fabric, then repeat.

There are now three threads across the shaded area, and the thread is on the outside edge of the wing. Now work a buttonhole bar from the outside edge to the inside edge. Remember not to catch in any of the fabric.

4 When the first bar is finished, work along to the second in chain stitch, and so on. Continue working in chain stitch along the inner wing edge until the second bar is reached and repeat for a buttonhole bar. When the wings have been outlined and all the bars worked, you can, if you prefer, remove the ring frame

although it is better to retain it if possible.

Working the embroidery Thread the needle with three strands of stranded cotton and work buttonhole stitches all round the areas to be cut.

5 When working the body, buttonhole round one half until you reach the crossover point. Fill the crossed area with satin stitch, making sure when you start to buttonhole again that the knots are on the edge to be cut.

The wing spots are worked in the same way – outlined in running stitch, then chain stitch, and finally buttonholing with the knots at the inside of the shape.

6 The head, wing stripes and

antennae are worked in interlaced backstitch. First work two rows of backstitch about 3mm/⅛in apart, using the coton à broder. The stitches must be small and regular and staggered across the parallel rows.

7 Thread the tapestry needle with two strands of stranded cotton and work herringbone stitch between the two rows of backstitch. The needle passes under the stitches without piercing the fabric at all. Anchor all threads securely and trim any ends.

Take the work out of the frame if you have used one and carefully cut away the fabric in the shaded areas. Hem the edges of the tablecloth by hand.

Alternative trace patterns

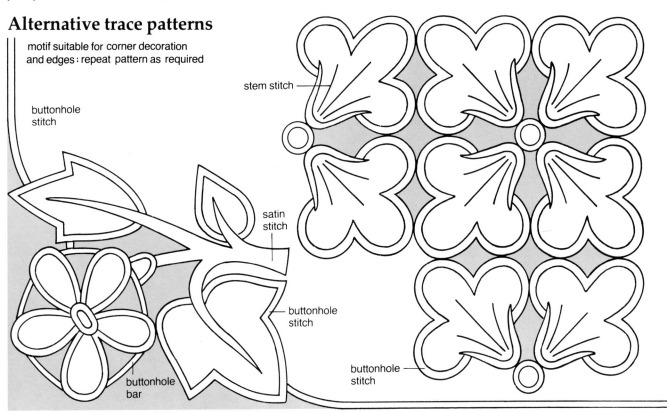

motif suitable for corner decoration and edges: repeat pattern as required

stem stitch

buttonhole stitch

satin stitch

buttonhole stitch

buttonhole bar

buttonhole stitch

buttonhole stitch

CHAPTER 13

Decorative borders in drawn thread work

Use this openwork technique to form decorative borders on household furnishings or to add a panel to a shirt front or a band round the hem of a skirt. The linen mats given in this chapter are laced with narrow satin ribbon and are ideal for a dressing table.

Drawn thread work is a type of counted-thread embroidery which can also be looked on as openwork. You first remove the warp or weft threads from an evenweave embroidery fabric leaving a series of threads running in one direction only. You then work embroidery stitches over these threads, forming decorative bands and borders. The technique is ideal for adorning table linen and, occasionally, panels on clothing – add extra embroidery to the work to create a harmonious piece.

Drawn thread stitches

The most useful basic stitch for drawn thread work is hemstitch. As the name suggests, it makes a neat, pretty hem on evenweave fabric, or you can simply use it for decorating the edges of a border cut within an area of fabric.

You must work each stitch over a fixed number of vertical fabric threads, usually between two and five. The stitches bunch these threads into groups. It is important to plan the work so that the length of border to be worked has a number of vertical threads exactly divisible by the number covered in each stitch.

Apart from simple hemstitch, there are variations such as ladder hemstitch, where both sides of a border are hemstitched over the same vertical threads, and interlaced hemstitch, where a thread is passed through the loose centre threads so they twist round each other in pairs.

Below: Drawn thread borders are much simpler to work than they look, and create beautiful, delicate designs on items like these matching dressing table mats in yellow and white.

Cutting and withdrawing the threads

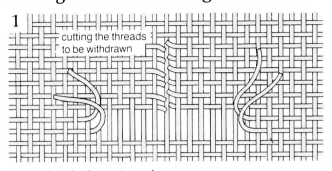

1 Decide which section of horizontal threads is to be withdrawn from the fabric and cut through them carefully at the centre of the open area using a pair of

sharp embroidery scissors. Unpick cut threads using a tapestry needle.
2 You can either fasten the ends with neat backstitches on the wrong side, or you can remove alternate

threads completely and darn the remaining threads back into the spaces in the fabric for at least 2.5cm/1in before trimming. This gives a secure, invisible finish.

Hemstitch

Prepare an open border by withdrawing the chosen number of horizontal threads and finishing off. Work from the wrong or right side, depending on which effect you prefer. This stitch can be worked from left to right as well as from right to left. This is how to work from right to left.
1 Secure the thread neatly and bring the needle up at the right-hand end of the border, two threads down from the edge. Pass the needle behind two or however many vertical threads you are

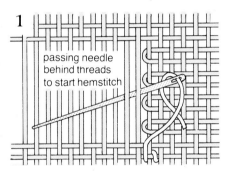

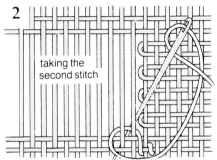

grouping in each stitch.
2 Pass the needle back across these vertical threads, round to the back of the fabric, emerging two threads (or three, four etc) to left of where it

first came up through the fabric. Repeat along the row. When you reach the end of the border, finish off the thread by passing it through last few stitches and snipping off.

Ladder hemstitch

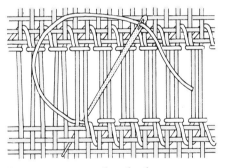

Prepare an open border by withdrawing the chosen number of horizontal threads and finishing off. Work a row of hemstitch, gathering the vertical threads into groups of two, three, or however many you wish. Now work along the opposite side of the border, stitching over the same groups of threads as on the opposite row.
Drawing the threads together on both sides makes them look like ladder rungs.

Interlaced hemstitch

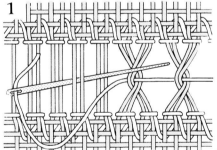

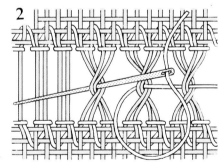

Having worked a border of ladder hemstitch, there are several ways of adding knotted or twisted patterns to the vertical threads in the centre. One of the commonest is interlaced hemstitch – a pretty variation which is simple and quick to work. Working from right to left, adjoining groups of threads are twisted around each other in pairs and held in place by a central thread.
1 Secure the thread halfway up the right-hand end of the open border. With the needle pointing from left

to right, pass it under the second group of threads, and over the first.
2 Bring the needle eye up and over so that the needle now points from right to left, and the first group of threads has been brought under the second one. Pull the thread through tightly to hold the twisted fabric threads in place. Treat the next two groups of threads in the same way and continue along the row, making sure you keep the central thread straight and taut. Secure it neatly at the end of the border.

Drawn thread work mats

This delightful set of three mats has drawn thread work borders, satin stitch embroidery and a ribbon trim. Practical as well as pretty, when the mats are used on a highly-polished wood surface they will prevent your trinkets, vases and cosmetics from scratching the surface while the dark grain of the wood shows off the delicate twisted thread pattern.

Although the decorative hemstitches given on pages 61 and 63 are worked using stranded cotton which matches the evenweave linen of the mats, you may prefer to experiment with different coloured cottons which contrast with the background fabric you are using. Work with three or more strands in the needle to obtain a colourful effect.

You will need
Coats Anchor stranded cotton,
  2 skeins each gorse yellow 0301,
  buttercup 0293, cream 0386 and
  white 0402
30cm/⅜yd white evenweave fabric,
  21 threads to 2.5cm/1in (width
  150cm/60in)
4.80m/5¼yd Offray white double-
  face satin ribbon width 3mm/⅛in
Tapestry needles size 20 and 24

Preparing the fabric
The width of the large mat is equal to each of the sides of the square mats. It is well worth taking the trouble to prepare the pieces of fabric carefully and count the threads accurately.
Cut one piece 43cm×24cm/ 17in×9½in and two pieces 24cm×24cm/9½in×9½in. Mark the centre line of each piece of fabric in both directions with a row of tacking stitches. The position of the drawn thread borders is determined by counting threads outwards from the centre. The layout diagram

shows the lower left-hand quarter of both the oblong and square mats and gives the numbers of fabric threads between the centres and the borders. The broken lines YY indicate the centre lines of the oblong mat, and YZ are the centre lines of the square mats. All numerals denote numbers of threads and the bracketed numerals show the number of threads which have been withdrawn.

Working the oblong mat
With one long side of the fabric facing, and following the layout diagram, cut through twelve horizontal threads at the centre. Prepare the left-hand half of the border first. Withdraw every *alternate* cut thread completely. Now withdraw the remaining threads back 128 threads to the left, darn the loose ends invisibly into the spaces left by the threads removed and trim. Complete the right-hand side of the border in the same way.
Repeat the procedure on the other three sides of the mat, following the layout diagram, until you have cut and finished off the four borders.
Begin hemstitching at the centre tacking line on one long side. Using three strands of white stranded cotton and size 24 needle, work ladder hemstitch on the right side over groups of two threads on all long edges of the open borders. The two long borders should have 128 pairs of threads, the two short borders 48 pairs. The arrangement of stitches at each corner is shown in the diagram.
Satin stitch Using the full six strands of thread and size 20

Below: Tie neat ribbon bows at the corners and snip diagonally across the ends.

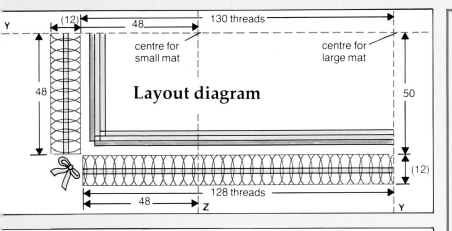

Layout diagram

(12)   48   130 threads

centre for small mat   centre for large mat

48   50

(12)

48   128 threads

Y   Z   Y

Stitching guide

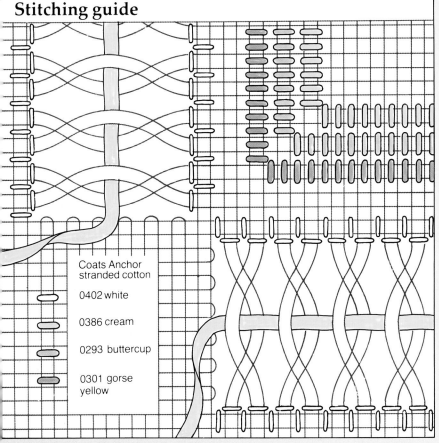

Coats Anchor stranded cotton

0402 white

0386 cream

0293 buttercup

0301 gorse yellow

Hemstitch variation

Here is another decorative variation on basic hemstitch which can be substituted for the borders used on the mats.

Working Italian hemstitch
Withdraw threads from the fabric for the required width, miss the required number of threads and withdraw another band of the same number of threads as first.
1 Bring the needle out two vertical threads to the left (or the required number) in the upper band of drawn threads; pass the needle round and behind these two threads, bringing it out where the needle first emerged.
2 Pass the needle diagonally across the fabric and behind and round the next two threads in the lower band, emerging two threads up and two threads to the left in the upper band, ready for next stitch. Repeat steps.

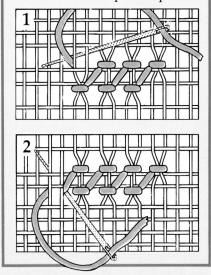

needle, work three bands of satin stitch – each band over two fabric threads – in the colours shown. The dark yellow is on the outside, then paler yellow, then cream – leave two free threads between the hemstitching and the satin stitch as shown in the diagram.

Working the square mats
Following the layout diagram, cut, withdraw and darn in loose ends of the borders. Work ladder hemstitch in the same way as for the oblong mat, beginning at the centre of each border. Add the same satin stitch embroidery within the borders.

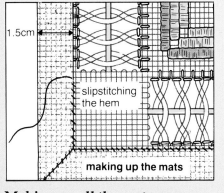

1.5cm

slipstitching the hem

making up the mats

Making up all the mats
Allow a 1.5cm/⅝in border between the drawn threadwork and the folded edge of each mat. Turn over

a double hem on the wrong side to the edge of the ladder hemstitch and slipstitch in place, mitring the corners.
Adding the ribbon trim Cut ten lengths of ribbon 36cm/14in long and two lengths 58cm/23in long. Thread each length of ribbon on to a needle and work interlaced hemstitch between all the hemstitched edges. Leave equal lengths of ribbon loose at each end to tie together in bows at the corners. The interlaced ribbon should be pulled firmly to lie in position through the centre of the twisted groups of threads.

CHAPTER 14

Lacy pulled thread stitches

*Pulled thread work is a form of counted thread embroidery
where the stitches are pulled tight, making
pretty, open patterns on the ground fabric. There's no need
to withdraw any threads and if you work
the stitches as fillings, the effect is beautiful.*

Some of the earliest existing pulled thread work comes from seventeenth century Italy. Decorative bands, probably from church linen, are worked in red or green silk threads on linen fabrics, using backgrounds of pulled thread stitches to surround plain motifs.

Eighteenth century pulled thread is lighter and more delicate and often worked in imitation of expensive lace. Satin stitch, shadow work and pulled work filling combined in pretty flower patterns adorn ladies' fichus, aprons and sleeve ruffles. Pulled work is also seen accompanied by English and trapunto quilting.

During the nineteenth century, the fine work develops into Ayrshire work but with more emphasis on the satin stitch motifs, and only a little filling. Pulled work is seen on European folk costume and household linens rather than on fashionable dress. Most of the work is bold and geometric on white or cream linens using matching thread.

The Scandinavian countries have carried on their peasant traditions today and use pulled work in both pictorial and geometric designs on their table linens and furnishings.

Choosing suitable materials

You can work pulled thread on any loosely-woven evenweave fabric using a matching or toning thread. Evenweave linen is best for table wear which needs to be washed regularly. For clothes or furnishings, you could use openly woven cotton or evenweave wool. The more open the weave, the lacier the finish. Some furnishing fabrics with a loose, open weave, or even hessian, can be suitable for pulled thread work.

Thread It's best to use a matching thread, or, if adding colours, be sure that they are not too bright and tone with the fabric. As each stitch has to

Framed cross filling

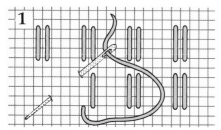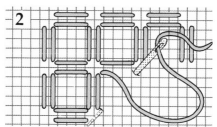

1 Work in pairs of satin stitches over four threads, leaving four threads between each pair. Pull all stitches tightly and leave one horizontal thread free between each row.

2 Now work horizontal rows of pairs of satin stitches (the other direction), again over four threads. As the stitches are pulled tightly, a cross appears in each hole.

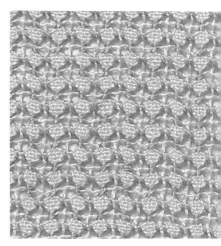

Satin stitch filling

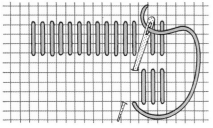

Work along the row in vertical satin stitch, each stitch over four horizontal threads. Pull each stitch tightly to draw the horizontal threads together, creating an open effect.

Honeycomb filling

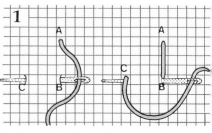

1 Working all stitches over four threads, bring the needle up at A, insert it at B and bring it out at C. Re-insert it at B, coming up at C to make a backstitch.

be pulled tight, the thread must be strong enough to stand the strain. Choose a thread of the same thickness as the fabric threads. Coton à broder, buttonhole twist, crochet cotton and pearl cotton are all good for pulled work. When using a coarse evenweave fabric, the unravelled warp threads can be used for the pulled work.

Always stretch the work in an embroidery hoop or frame. This makes it much easier to count threads when stitching and keep tension even. Darn all thread ends into the back of the work.

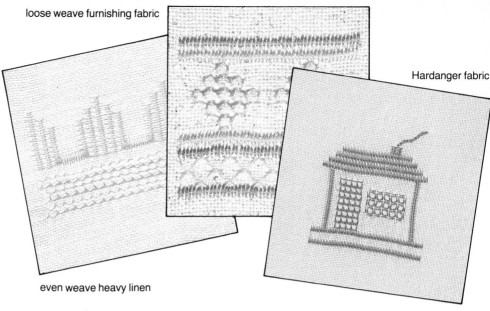

loose weave furnishing fabric

Hardanger fabric

even weave heavy linen

Designs

Geometric or pictorial designs are equally suitable for pulled thread work which is often used as a filling for motifs. Work the outline first in stem stitch, chain stitch or whipped chain stitch and fill in with the chosen pulled thread stitch.

Filling stitches

Most pulled thread stitches are worked from right to left, turning the work at the end of each row.

Begin the first row of the filling at the widest part of the motif, filling the motif on first one side of the first row, then the other. At the beginning and end of each row make part stitches against the outline to add strength. If the first stitch on the next row begins in the same hole as the last stitch of the previous row, take a small stitch through the back of the outline stitches on the wrong side of the work between the two stitches.

Four-sided filling

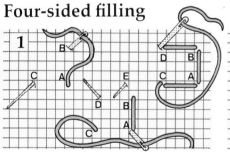

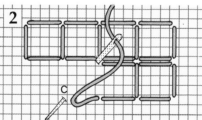

1 Working over four threads, bring the needle up at A, insert it at B and bring it out at C. Insert it again at A, bring out again at D. Next insert at B, bring out at C, and finally insert at D, bringing out at E ready for the next square.

2 Work in rows from right to left, turning the work at the end of each row. Pull all the stitches tight as you work. Notice how horizontal stitches share holes with adjacent stitches in the rows above and below.

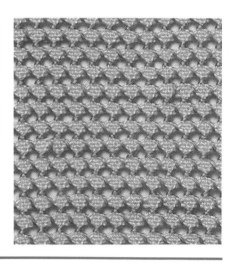

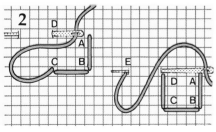

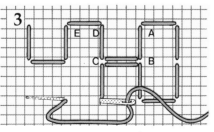

2 Insert the needle at D, bringing it out at E. Finally, insert it again at D, coming out at E to make the backstitch.

3 Work from right to left turning at the end of each row. As each stitch is pulled tight during working, the vertical stitches become slanted. The backstitches share holes with stitches in the rows above and below.

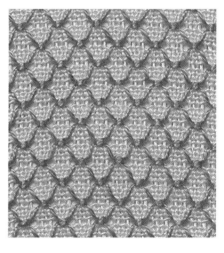

Café curtain with green leaf border

Above: Pulled thread filling stitches give a light, lacy look to simple motifs.

Fresh green leaf motifs in pulled thread work are the ideal decoration for a café curtain. An embroidered curtain like this one is the perfect answer when you need a half curtain, yet wish to add interest to a window The curtain shown here is made up in pure evenweave linen, but you could use an open-weave furnishing fabric.

You will need

For a curtain measuring 90cm/36in wide and up to 89cm/35in deep
1m/1yd white evenweave linen, width 140cm/54in, 20 threads to 2.5cm/1in
DMC pearl cotton No 5, 2 skeins each in 704 (mid green) and 966 (pale green) and 1 skein in 369 (very pale green)
Sewing thread to match fabric
20cm/8in diameter embroidery ring frame
Tapestry needle size 22
Dressmaker's carbon paper
Tracing paper
Plain paper
Hanging rod or wire

Preparing the fabric and working the embroidery

Trim the piece of fabric to 110cm/43in width and mark 10cm/4in in from each side edge with a row of contrasting tacking along the straight grain. (These form the finished curtain edges).

Tack a line across the fabric 15cm/6in up from the bottom edge then tack a line up the centre of the fabric.

Enlarge the leaf shape from the pattern below (1 square = 3cm/1¼in).

Using dressmaker's carbon paper, trace five leaf shapes across the lower edge of the fabric, spacing them evenly between the two outer lines of tacking and having the lower tip of each leaf two fabric threads above the lower line.

Working the embroidery

First outline each leaf motif in whipped chain stitch (page 48) using shade 704. (The central ribs are added after the pulled work fillings have been worked.)
Following the stitch scheme and with fabric stretched tightly, work the appropriate filling in each leaf

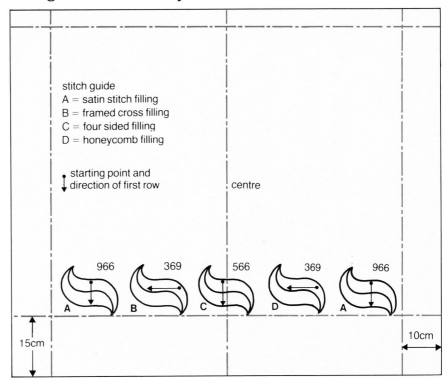

stitch guide
A = satin stitch filling
B = framed cross filling
C = four sided filling
D = honeycomb filling

• starting point and
↓ direction of first row

centre

966   369   566   369   966

A   B   C   D   A

15cm

10cm

shape. Begin the first row of the pattern across the widest part of each leaf as indicated.
When all the leaves are completed,

work the central rib of each in whipped chain stitch in shade 704. Steam-press the work on the wrong side.

Finishing off the curtain

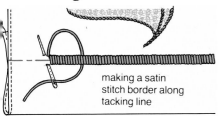

making a satin stitch border along tacking line

Remove central vertical tacking thread. Cut down each side of the curtain 2cm/¾in outside the tacked lines and press along tacked lines. Make narrow double hems along sides. Pin, tack and catch into place with the matching sewing thread. Remove tacking threads.
Fold lower hem to wrong side 6cm/2¼in below lower tacking line, pin and tack turning in place.
Using shade 704, make a counted satin stitch border over five threads along tacking line, making sure that each stitch passes through both layers of fabric. Trim away excess fabric on reverse, close to stitches. Trim and fold over fabric across the top of the curtain to make a casing at required position, for hanging. Pin, tack and hem in place. Press.

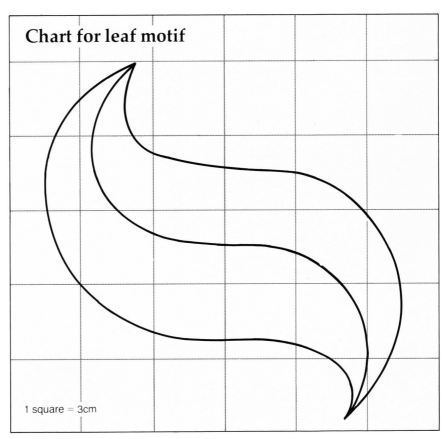

Chart for leaf motif

1 square = 3cm

CHAPTER 15

Decorative insertion stitches

*This technique originated long ago as a method of joining
narrow widths of fabric edge to edge.
The stitches are simple to work and look very professional
used to decorate bedlinen, lingerie or
added to clothes made from commercial patterns.*

In olden times, fabric could only be woven in narrow widths so for garments it was important to use a method of linking the strips that was less wasteful of fabric than conventional seams. Later on, these open seams joined with insertion stitches became part of the decoration of clothes and fine examples appear on the shirts of Elizabethan times.

Suitable fabrics and threads

Fine, firmly woven fabrics are the best choice for blouses and lingerie. When joining thicker fabrics use the plain, woven selvedges where possible. Insertion stitches can also be useful for joining pieces of leather and felt.

Single threads such as silk twist, pearl cotton, or coton à broder are the best for this kind of embroidery. Choose a thread which is a little heavier than the fabric to be used.

How to work open seams

It is essential to finish cut edges of woven fabrics with a rolled or narrow hem. Use tacking to hold this in place while the embroidery is in progress.

After turning the hems tack the fabrics to be joined to a strong paper backing, leaving the appropriate space between the two edges. This can vary from 5mm to 1.5cm/¼in to ⅝in according to the stitch being used. The embroidery stitches are worked through the fabric, but not through the paper. Begin and end your threads with a small backstitch worked into the back of the hem and be very careful to keep tension and spacing even throughout.

Faggoting

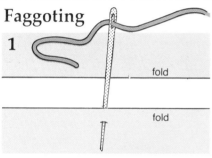

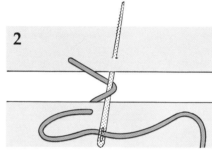

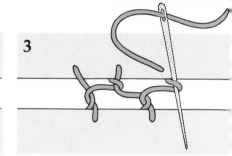

This is the most popular stitch for joining open seams, so it is often the general name given to the technique. Work from left to right.
1 Secure the thread to one side of the seam and take a stitch across to the other side, a little to the right. Always bring the needle through from below.
2 Pass the needle under then over the first stitch, twisting first left, then right, and take a stitch back to the first side, a little to the right.
3 Repeat steps 1 and 2 along the row, continuing until the seam is completed. Be careful to keep an even tension so as not to pucker fabric or threads.

Buttonhole insertion stitch

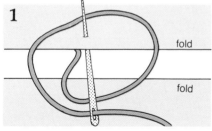

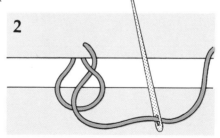

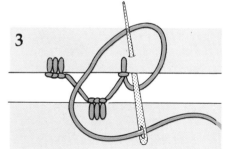

Use tailor's buttonhole stitch here – this produces a firmer knot. Again, work from left to right.
1 Secure thread to hem edge. Take the needle behind and up through the fabric with the thread looped under the eye and the point of the needle as shown.
2 Draw the thread through the fabric and give it a slight pull backwards towards the edge so that a small knot forms.
3 Work a group of two, three or four stitches close together. Then take the thread across to the other side of the seam, slightly to the right. Work a matching group on this side and continue along the row.

Right: This is an up-to-date example of an embroidery technique with an old-fashioned feel. A blouse yoke gives you a good, flat surface for insertion stitch decoration.

Knotted insertion stitch

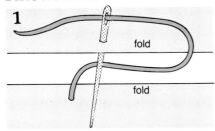 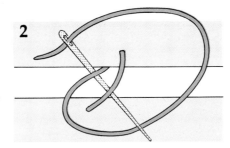 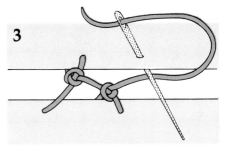

This is based on buttonhole stitch (page 21) and worked from left to right.
1 Bring the thread up through the lower edge and make a buttonhole stitch into the upper edge, so that the thread lies diagonally.
2 Make a second buttonhole stitch over the two threads, but not through the fabric, with the needle pointing diagonally towards the direction you are working.
3 Now make a buttonhole stitch in the lower edge and work a stitch over the threads only as before.

Laced insertion stitch

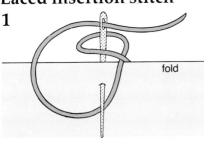 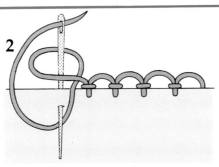 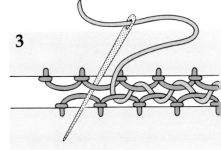

This is a favourite border stitch from Mexico. Braid edging stitch is worked along each hem edge and it is then laced together with a contrasting thread. Note that it is easier to work the edging stitch before tacking the pieces of fabric to the backing.
1 Working from right to left with the hem held away from you, bring the thread up from underneath the edge and make a loop as shown. Pass the needle down through the loop, bring it up through the fabric a little below the edge, and over the thread.
2 Pull the thread through to make a knot. Repeat steps 1 and 2 to make another knot, but pull the thread through loosely. Adjust the size of the loop between the knots. Pull the thread away from you to tighten the knot – practise the stitch to obtain even loops.
3 Work the second (opposite) edge in the same way. Line up the edges so that the loops lie alternately and tack fabric to the firm backing. Using a tapestry (blunt) needle, weave contrasting thread through the loops, from side to side as shown.

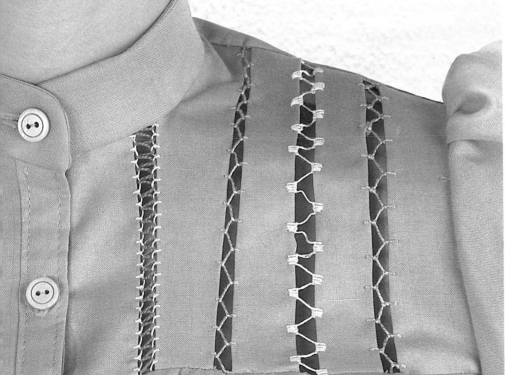

Faggotted blouse

Insertion stitches give a pretty open-work effect to parts of garments such as this yoked blouse. The pattern used here has a front opening but you could adapt the instructions slightly to work it on a one-piece yoke.

You will need
Paper pattern for a yoked blouse
Lightweight fabric according to pattern requirements
Matching sewing thread, buttons and other notions specified
1 skein each pearl cotton No 5, or coton à broder in 3 shades
Strong paper, tracing paper, set square, ruler and pencil
Embroidery and tapestry needles

Left: Use this photograph as your guide to placing the various stitches.

Preparing the yoke for embroidery

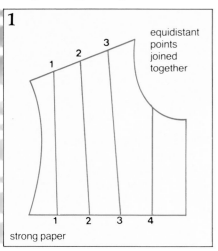

1 equidistant points joined together

strong paper

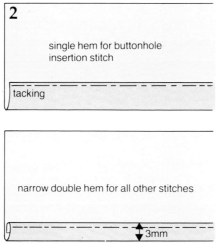

2 single hem for buttonhole insertion stitch

tacking

narrow double hem for all other stitches

3mm

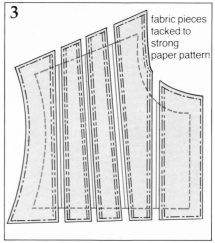

3 fabric pieces tacked to strong paper pattern

Trace the pattern for the front yoke on to strong paper. Draw both right and left sides.

1 Mark four equidistant points along the seamline of the bottom edge of each yoke. Mark three equidistant points along the shoulder seamline. Join the three outer points on the bottom to the three points on the shoulder. Using a set square to obtain a right angle draw a vertical line from the fourth point to the neck edge. Trace these four lines on to the original pattern tissue. Cut all

round the pattern, along the *seamline*. Pin the pattern to a double thickness of fabric and, leaving a generous seam allowance, cut out. Mark the seamline on both sides of the fabric with tacking or fabric pencil. Mark the seamline where the four lines meet it along base and shoulder edge. Unpin the pattern and join the top and bottom marks using a ruler and fabric pencil. Cut along these lines so that the right and left yokes are each in five pieces.

2 Turn under and tack narrow hems

along all the cut edges. Use double hems which should not exceed 3mm/⅛in on all except the hems for the buttonhole insertion stitch, which only need to be turned under once. Depending on the fabric, you may need to make your hems slightly wider.

3 Tack each piece of yoke on to the strong paper pattern, matching the seamlines. The vertical lines ruled on the pattern should be midway between the hemmed fabric edges. The yoke is now ready for working the embroidery.

Working the embroidery

Distribute your thread colours evenly – if you have chosen white, remember that it shows up the best, so use it for the finer-looking stitches. Use two different colours for the laced insertion stitch.

Referring to the photograph (below left), work laced insertion (two shades) nearest the centre fronts, then faggoting, buttonhole insertion and knotted insertion nearest the armhole. Use one

thickness of the thread, and begin and end your stitching well outside the top and bottom seamlines. Remove the work from the backing and take out the tacking stitches which are holding the hems. Press.

Making up the blouse

Cut out the remaining blouse pieces. Join the back yoke (if the pattern includes one) to the blouse back.

Pin and tack the front yokes to the blouse fronts, ready for joining with a French seam. Match edges carefully so that front yoke pieces are kept well apart. Tack both stages of the seam securely to make sure of a neat finish. Press seam away from yoke and catch down invisibly on front. Join front and back yokes at shoulder seams in the same way, pressing seams away from front yokes.

Finish the making up according to the pattern instructions.

DESIGN EXTRA

Insertion stitch ideas

Insertion stitches, particularly faggoting, have traditionally been used on household linens. They make an attractive finish for blouses – try an openwork border

down either side of the buttonband, or rows of stitches down the length of sleeves. The same idea adapts prettily to nighties and petticoats.

CHAPTER 16

Machine embroidery

If you can stitch in a straight line, you can do machine embroidery. Simple patterns are possible using a straight stitch but a swing needle can achieve more ambitious effects. Practise stitch and colour combinations and brighten up a plain skirt hem.

You can use machine embroidery to make a variety of decorative effects on clothes, accessories and household linens. Striking patterns can be achieved using simple lines of straight and zigzag stitches and detailed pictorial and abstract designs are possible as you become more skilful at using the machine.

Below: Plain and random thread machine patterns including a straight stitch pattern, satin stitch, a mirror image hearts border, a twin needle wavy line and a row of machine tailor's tacks.

Freestyle machine embroidery is the most complicated technique and is worked without the presser foot and feed dog (metal teeth in the needle plate).

What kind of machine?

Any sewing machine can be used for decorative stitching but, of course, the more basic the machine, the smaller the range of patterns which are possible.

Straight stitch machines By varying the length of the stitch and by moving the fabric in different directions,

pivoting at corners with the needle in the fabric, you can create a limited range of simple stitch patterns.
Leave the presser foot in the raised position when working in this way.

Swing needle machines By setting a short stitch length to make a close zigzag, and adjusting the stitch width, you can make wide or narrow bands of satin stitch. By lengthening the stitch but keeping a wide setting the zigzag elongates, reducing the density of thread on the surface of the fabric. Experiment with stitch lengths from the shortest to the longest that your machine can do.

The closer the zigzag, the slower the fabric moves under the machine foot. Take care not to force the fabric through or you will get an uneven effect.

A twin needle can stitch many pretty double patterns using two different colours of thread for a variegated look. Remember not to set too long or wide a stitch – you could damage the needles if they strike the footplate.

Embroidery stitch feature Some of today's sophisticated electronic sewing machines offer up to thirty stitch patterns. Apart from the usual straight and zigzag stitches, they can sew scallops, triangles, leaves, feather stitch – even little trains for childrens' clothes.

Obviously your innovative abilities do not have to be so great – much of the credit for the decorative results will pass to the machine. There is, however, quite an art in choosing pattern and colour combinations.

In general, you need to decrease tension for decorative stitches of this kind to prevent the fabric from puckering. If it still puckers, try decreasing the tension on the upper thread even more.

Fabrics and threads

As with all types of embroidery, it is a good idea to match the composition of thread to fabric – silk with silk, cotton with cotton, etc.

Adapt the thickness of the needle and thread to the weight of the fabric as you would for normal machine sewing. Light and open weave fabrics may be difficult to embroider without the fabric puckering. Tissue

Right: Finish off all loose threads at the back of the work or they may unravel when the skirt is washed.

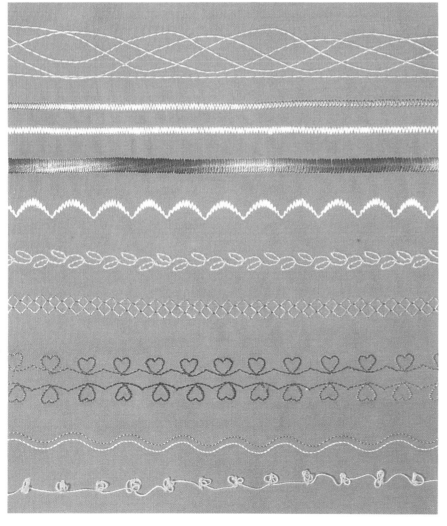

paper pinned beneath the fabric helps – just tear it away after stitching. The more complicated the stitch, the more thread it will use – satin stitch, in particular, uses up a great deal of thread so make sure you have sufficient before you start.

Special cotton thread in a large range of colours is sold for machine embroidery, including some random dyed shades which gradually change colour, but ordinary cotton machine twist is perfectly suitable.

Embroidery threads such as pearl cotton look very pretty and give greater emphasis to the pattern as

they are more loosely twisted than regular thread. Other alternatives are silk twist which comes in glowing shades and metallic threads which are fun to use.

All these thicker threads must be wound on to the bobbin as they cannot be used as the top thread. Work the embroidery on the *wrong* side of the fabric so that the decorative thread appears on the right side.

You may need to alter the tension on the machine so that the lower, thicker thread is held in position by the upper thread and not pulled through the fabric.

Patterns and stitches

Successful machine embroidery is the result of experimentation. Do try out the effects to see if the colours and stitches work well together and to check that the fabric is suitable. Consult your machine manual for any specific suggestions regarding needle size, tension adjustment, needle position, stitch length, and so on. Try as many different settings on your machine as possible.

Remember that simple embroidery can often be more effective than more complicated patterns so don't be too ambitious to start with.

Machine embroidery on a skirt hem and matching shawl

A few rows of very basic machine embroidery have made the plain cotton dirndl skirt and shawl (shown on the previous page) into something special. By matching tops and accessories with the stitchery on the skirt, you can create a lovely co-ordinating outfit. Although a machine with embroidery features was used, most of the stitching was done with zigzag, using different stitch settings.

The skirt hem

A plain white cotton skirt was chosen but the same colourful embroidery would look equally good on a black skirt.

satin stitch blocks

zigzag diagonals

row 7

6
5
4
3
2
1

You will need

Plain cotton skirt
3 reels of three different shades of cotton thread (this is sufficient for both skirt and shawl)
Dressmaker's chalk pencil

Preparing the skirt

The first band of embroidery lies 2.5cm/1in from the lower edge of the skirt. Measuring carefully, mark this line at intervals with a dressmaker's chalk pencil. Practise on spare fabric to obtain a close satin stitch band.

Working the embroidery

Row 1 Beginning at one of the skirt seams, or one of the front edges if it is a button-through skirt, work close satin stitch all the way round to give a strong defined edge.

Row 2 Mark a second chalk line,

Matching shawl

To complete the outfit make this easy shawl, it is simply made from a triangle of fabric.

You will need

1m/1⅛yd of 112cm/44in wide light cotton fabric to match or contrast with skirt
1 reel of three different shades of cotton thread

Stitching the shawl

Trim the 112cm/44in side of the piece of fabric to 100cm/40in to make a square. Cut the fabric in half diagonally and tack a double 8mm/ ⅜in hem along all three edges.

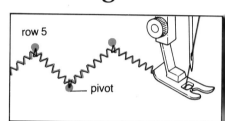

6mm/¼in away from the edge of the satin stitch. Stitch along this row in your second colour, using the same width of stitch, but with a longer stitch setting to give a more open zigzag.

Row 3 With the same colour in the needle, shorten the stitch length slightly to give an effect halfway between the first and second rows, and stitch a third row, again 6mm/ ¼in away from the second row.

Row 4 Now repeat the stitch length of the second row, still keeping the second colour in the needle.

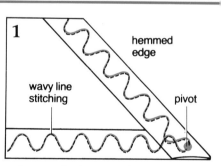

1 Secure the hem with a row of decorative stitching, using a zigzag stitch variation or a wavy line.

2 Follow this with another two rows, keeping 6mm/¼in between the rows as on the skirt. You can use satin stitch, and machine blind stitch as here, or any other you like.

Machine embroidery tips

Before you start, clean the machine with a soft cloth to remove any excess oil and lint which could spoil your work.

Press the fabric to be embroidered so that it is completely smooth.

Mark stitching lines and patterns on the fabric with dressmaker's chalk pencil and brush it off afterwards.

After completing a line of stitching, leave an end on the right side long enough to be threaded through to the wrong side afterwards. When the embroidery is complete, knot all ends securely and trim off.

Row 5 Change to your third colour to work a row of a decorative stitch such as the scallop used here. If you don't have a machine with an embroidery feature, try using a medium zigzag stitch to make a chevron pattern, pivoting the fabric at each point.

Rows 6 and 7 Repeat the second row in the second colour before finishing off with another band of dense satin stitch in the third colour.

Diagonals and blocks The rest of the design is formed with a series of parallel diagonal lines in a medium zigzag stitch and each line is surmounted by two little satin stitch blocks. The 9cm/3½in diagonal lines are 4cm/1½in apart and slant at about 45°. Mark them on the skirt using a ruler and dressmaker's chalk. Practise working satin stitch blocks. Try to form neat 6mm/¼in squares about 6mm/¼in apart.

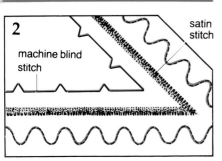

Be careful to pivot the fabric neatly at the corners of the shawl.

If you are enjoying your stitching, you can continue adding as many rows as you like. For an extra professional look, decorate the waistband of the skirt, echoing the design used round the shawl.

Machine embroidery for a personal touch

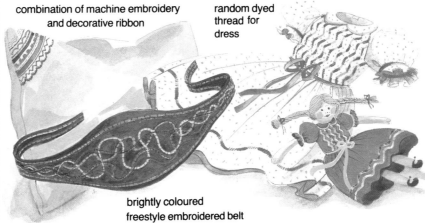

combination of machine embroidery and decorative ribbon

random dyed thread for dress

brightly coloured freestyle embroidered belt

Add a finishing touch to purchased items or things you have sewn yourself. The effect you achieve can either be subtle or bold. This is determined by your choice of colours and stitches.

Personalize anything from a plain hanky to collars, cuffs, pockets, sash belts, dress yokes, aprons, sheets, pillowcases and tablecloths. Little girls' plain skirts can be given a really festive look with some bright machine embroidery.

Try geometric designs on tablecloths and napkins – use a zigzag satin stitch for this. Scatter the cloth with boxes, squiggles and triangles to match your other furnishings. Try out some of the random-dyed threads in pastel colours. These also look stunning on the yoke of a plain white cotton dress, or used in a pretty scallop trim for a baby's dress.

Below: Design a set of linen table napkins with coloured lines and squiggles to match a plain cloth.

CHAPTER 17

Freestyle machining to create a picture

Machine embroidery can achieve very professional results using a swing needle machine which is capable of free stitching without the feed dog. Two stitch techniques and a glowing range of machine embroidery threads were used to work these charming duck pictures.

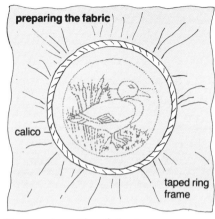

preparing the fabric

calico

taped ring frame

Use freestyle machine embroidery to achieve a pictorial effect which is more flexible and creative than the simple stitches used in the last chapter. Instead of using the machine with the feed dog and the presser foot in their normal positions, the feed dog must be lowered or covered and the presser foot removed so that the fabric can be moved freely in all directions. With the machine set to zigzag an all-over long and short stitch effect is produced.

Preparing the machine

As with all machine embroidery, freestyle work uses up a lot of thread, so always begin with a full bobbin. Lower the feed dog (or cover with the special plate provided) and remove the presser foot. Lower the presser foot lever before beginning to stitch to maintain the necessary tension. Set the top thread tension to low – usually 3 – but this can vary slightly with different models. It is important that the bobbin thread does not come up to the fabric surface while stitching. If it does, loosen the top tension a little more.

Set a short stitch length and the stitch width at No 4 and thread up the machine. You can use any colour except black in the bobbin.

Preparing the fabric

Firmly woven calico is one of the best fabrics to choose for machine embroidery. Mark the design on to the fabric, choosing a suitable transfer method (page 10). Then mount the fabric in a prepared ring frame, no larger than 20cm/8in diameter. The small ring is on top of the fabric. To do this, lay fabric right side up over large ring, bind small ring with tape and push it in so that fabric is very taut. The fabric should lie absolutely flat on the footplate for stitching. Take care that the grain of the fabric is straight and the design is placed centrally in the frame.

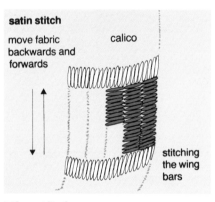

satin stitch

move fabric backwards and forwards

calico

stitching the wing bars

The stitches

Two basic stitching techniques are used to stitch pictures like the ones in this chapter.

Satin stitch This can be made to resemble hand-worked satin stitch. The stitches should lie very close to each other and by going over the same row twice, you can produce a dense, raised effect.

Move the ring frame backwards or forwards as you stitch. The quicker you do this, the more widely spaced the stitches will be. Use this stitch to work solid blocks of colour or the more linear parts of the design.

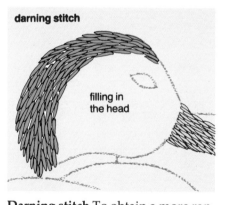

darning stitch

filling in the head

Darning stitch To obtain a more random effect, move the ring frame from side to side at the same time as backwards or forwards. Quicker movements will produce wider stitches. Use this stitch for filling larger areas of the design with a textured look.

For both stitch effects, aim to keep the fabric moving continuously to avoid lumps of thread clogging the machine. Remember to keep your fingers well away from the needle when stitching – it is not protected by the presser foot.

At stages throughout the embroidery, it is a good idea to remove the frame from the machine and tidy loose ends on both sides of the fabric by taking top threads through to the back with a crewel needle and tying each group of threads in a knot. Cut off the ends.

Starting to machine

Thread up the machine with your chosen colour and bring the needle down into the fabric by moving the balance wheel towards you. Holding the top (needle) thread, stitch until the bobbin thread comes up to the top and pull through.

Start to machine steadily, following the lines of the design and moving the fabric in the frame by hand.

When you have finished a section, raise the needle from the fabric by moving the balance wheel away from you, and remove the embroidery. Cut both threads, leaving about 15cm/6in to be finished off later.

Practise both satin stitch and darning stitch, moving the frame in all directions and experimenting with different effects until you can embroider confidently.

Duck and drake machine-embroidered pictures

These charming pictures of a pair of mallard ducks set in landscapes each measure 15cm/6in across. Special machine-embroidery thread in glowing colours has been used, including two random-dyed colours which give a lovely mottled effect to the sky and the duck's wings. Work slowly and carefully, practising with each new colour to obtain the best effect for the area you are stitching. Try to consider the direction of the feathers and the way the grass grows to achieve a realistic effect when stitching.

You will need

2 pieces of medium-weight unbleached calico, 30cm/12in square
Orange dressmaker's carbon paper
Tracing paper
19cm/7½in ring frame
Sewing machine needles No 11 (90)
Crewel needle
DMC machine-embroidery thread Brillanté d'Alsace No 30 in shades 5200, 783, 699, 796, 434, 898, 415, 105, 741, 93, 580, 711, 344, 644, 368, 437
Machine-embroidery thread No 30 for bobbin (any colour except black)
DMC stranded cotton – 1 skein each in 989, 741, 367, 3371 and white
2 circles of stiff backing card (diameter of picture plus frame rebate)
2 16cm/6¼in diameter frames with rebates (circular)
Buttonhole thread and needle for mounting and stretching work

Above: If you have difficulty obtaining round frames or would prefer a square picture, either continue the landscape to fill the square area or have the circular embroidery framed in a square-edged mount.

Preparing to embroider

Trace the main duck and drake outlines from the life-size photographs on the next two pages. Use dressmaker's carbon paper to transfer the design on to the fabric. Mount the marked area of the calico in the ring frame and work the stitching using the stitch guide and the colour key.
Work the stitchery in the order given in the stitch guide; the drake is worked first and the duck instructions refer back as necessary.

Working the drake

1 First, stitch the white collar from the back to the front of the neck – a single row of satin stitch.
2 Embroider the two white parts of the wing bar with close satin stitch.
3 Work the white tail with close darning stitch.
4 The drake's beak and eye area should be filled in next, using darning stitch.
5 Now fill in the green head area, following the contours of the head with darning stitch and blending the stitches into the white collar.
6 Add the blue wing bar using five rows of close satin stitch at right angles to the white feathers on the wing bar.
7 Use darning stitch to work the brown tail feathers above and below the white feathers. You may need to operate the machine manually to achieve the curves on the tail.
8 Embroider the chest area and the bottom wing feathers below the blue and white bars in darning stitch.
9 The grey underpart is also worked in darning stitch, following

contours as for the head and chest.
10 Change to the random-dyed thread to stitch the back and upper wing area with darning stitch. Guide the ring frame in a series of V-shapes so that your stitching looks like feathers. You may need to practise on a spare scrap of fabric.
11 Work the webbed areas of the feet in darning stitch and then the legs and toes in a close satin stitch. Taper the stitch width as you get towards the toes.
12 Now stitch the sky using the random-dyed blue thread and darning stitch with a horizontal movement. Do not forget to leave a space for the bulrush.
13 The lake is embroidered in two steps. First stitch some light blue reflections with a widely-spaced darning stitch then set a close darning stitch and fill the remaining water area in grey.
14 The main area of grass is done

with darning stitch. Turn the ring frame so that the drake is facing you and stitch with quick vertical movements so that the stitches are long and random, overlapping the sky and lake area.
15 Embroider the bulrush leaves in close darning stitch, the stalks in a row of vertical satin stitch (stitch width 1.5), and the seedheads with a vertical row of satin stitch (stitch width 4). Go over this row twice. Remove work from the machine.
The hand embroidery To add texture and depth to the picture, add a few simple stitches worked in two strands of stranded cotton thread.

The pupil of the drake's eye is worked as a double French knot. To work the reeds, make several long stitches, 1-2cm/½-¾in in length. For daisies, make double French knots for the centres and tiny straight stitches for the petals.

Trace for drake

shade nos

☐ 5200
☐ 783
☐ 699
☐ 796
☐ 434
☐ 898
☐ 415
☐ 105
☐ 741
☐ 93
☐ 580
☐ 344
☐ 644
☐ 368
☐ 437

DMC machine embroidery thread Brillanté d'Alsace No 30 shade numbers

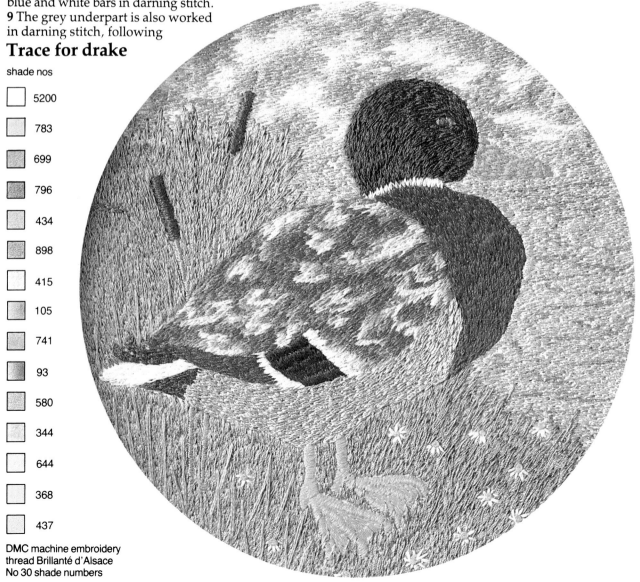

Trace for duck

shade nos

- 5200
- 796
- 898
- 105
- 741
- 93
- 344
- 644
- 368
- 711

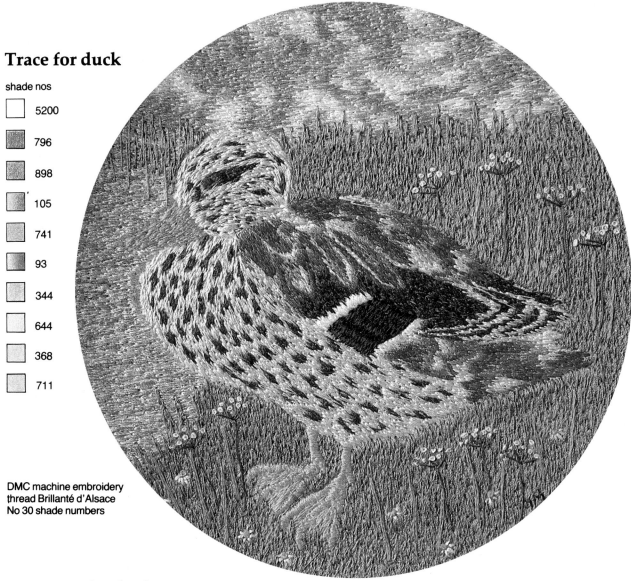

DMC machine embroidery
thread Brillanté d'Alsace
No 30 shade numbers

Working the duck

1 Stitch two white wing bars as for the drake, using two single rows of satin stitch. Add five rows of dark blue close satin stitch at right angles to the white feathers, between them.

2 Work the beak and eye as for the drake.

3 The head and chest dark areas are stitched next – fill in the dark area round the eye and small groups of darning stitch for the dark parts of the mottled head and chest. Continue with dark brown thread to embroider the dark areas of the wing, including a series of large V-shapes towards the back.

4 Now fill in the light areas of the head and chest, also the light areas of the wing. Alternate the V-shapes with the dark ones.

5 The whole of the back and tail are stitched with the random brown thread, again guiding the ring frame to simulate the features.

6 Fill in the webbed feet as before, then the legs and toes.

7 The sky is the same as for the first picture, as are the lake and grass. Remove embroidery from machine.
The hand embroidery Add reeds

Finishing off

Remove each embroidery from the ring frame and press with a steam iron on the wrong side. Turn over and press under a damp cloth. Never iron directly on to the embroidery as this will make it shiny.

Mounting and stretching Mark a 28cm/11in circle on the calico to give a 6.5cm/2½in border round the embroidery. Cut away excess fabric. Place card circle on wrong side of embroidery. Thread a strong needle with buttonhole twist. Make a firm knot and take a small stitch about 1cm/½in in from the edge of the calico. Lace tightly back and forth

and daisies exactly as before. To stitch cow parsley, make one long green stitch for the stalk and five smaller ones at the top. With one strand of white thread, stitch French knots for the flower heads.

mounting and stretching

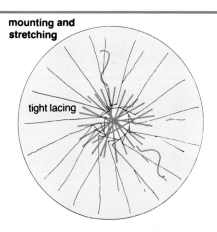

tight lacing

across the card, making tucks where necessary. Have the embroidery framed, or frame it yourself.

CHAPTER 18

Mock smocking adds a special touch

Smocking is not just a decoration for babies and children's clothes – give a unique designer touch to your own blouse or shirtdress with bands of elegant smocking. Using a quick technique called mock smocking you can smock pretty collars and cuffs in no time.

Smocking is the technique of gathering fabric with rows of decorative stitching, giving it elasticity and fullness.

The earliest existing English examples are the wonderful country smocks of the 19th century on which intricate smocking incorporates extra embroidery stitches – chain stitch, feather stitch and buttonhole.

Smocked dresses were introduced in the 1880's and have remained firm favourites in babies' and childrens' wardrobes ever since.

Fabrics and threads

Any fabric which can be gathered satisfactorily can be smocked. Among the most suitable are cotton lawn, voile, fine wool, and cotton/wool mixtures.

Some fabrics have built-in smocking guides in their construction or design – a regular marking which enables them to be gathered up evenly. Needlecord, checked, striped or spotted fabrics and obvious even-weaves like hessian all fall in to this category.

Plain fabrics need extra preparation – the addition of smocking dots as a guide.

When smocking a printed fabric, make sure that the print and the smocking stitches enhance each other. Match the smocking thread to the weight of the fabric; single twisted threads such as pearl cotton, coton à broder, silk twist, linen thread, or even crochet cotton are best. Choose a thread which tones with the ground fabric, or picks out a colour from a striped or printed fabric.

Use crewel needles in fine sizes.

Marking fabric for smocking

Smocking is always worked on the fabric before cutting out and making up the garment.

Real smocking is worked on fabric which has first been gathered up evenly into tubes and requires about three times the finished width of fabric. In mock smocking (see below) the fabric is gathered as it is being smocked. In either case, the fabric needs to be marked with regularly spaced dots (unless it has a built-in guide – such as stripes) so that the gathers are neat and even.

Printed transfers of smocking dots in various sizes, obtainable from needlework shops, are transferred by ironing them on to the wrong side of the work.

Mock smocking

This type of smocking is not as strong as real smocking, so it should only be used as decoration.

However, it looks like real smocking and is quicker to work – smocking and gathering are done in one step. The smocking dots are transferred on to the *right* side of the fabric.

To do mock smocking you need only twice the finished width of fabric so it does not produce the fullness of real smocking. It is therefore often used for thicker fabrics such as corduroy. Even knitting, which would become very bulky if smocked by the traditional method, can be mock smocked successfully.

All the smocking stitches can be worked in the usual way, picking up dots (instead of tubes of fabric as on real smocking), and pulling each stitch tight, to gather up the fabric.

Two basic mock smocking stitches are shown here – cable stitch and surface honeycomb stitch.

Any edges not to be enclosed in a seam need to be neatened before you begin the smocking.

Mock cable stitch

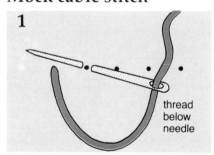

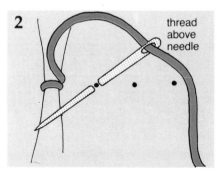
thread below needle

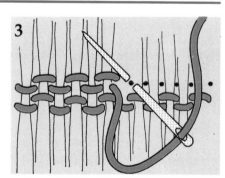
thread above needle

This pretty stitch is worked along a single row of dots.
Bring the needle out at the first dot, on the left-hand side of the row.
1 With the thread lying below the needle, pick up the next dot with the needle running from right to left. Pull thread to gather the fabric.

2 Now pick up the next dot with the thread lying above the needle. Continue along the row, placing the thread alternately below and above the needle. Make sure that all your gathers are even – giving the work the occasional pull from top to bottom to regulate the gathers.

3 Work the next row along the row of dots immediately below, turning the work so that you are still working from left to right and the worked row is beneath the dots you are stitching over.

Mock surface honeycomb stitch

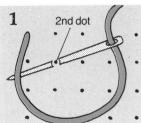

1

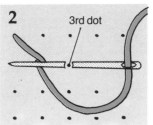

2

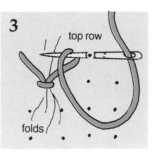

3

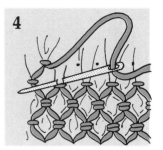

4

1 Working from left to right, bring the needle out at the first dot on the top row and make a small backstitch.
Now pick up the dot diagonally below to the right, with the needle running from right to left, and pull through. Pull these up and down stitches only slightly.

2 With your next stitch, pick up the next right-hand dot. The needle should still run from right to left. Pull tight to draw up the fabric, which forms two small folds.
Make sure you use every dot, taking the thread vertically up and down.

3 Now pick up the next dot on the top row so that the thread is taken round the right-hand fold. Join this dot to its right-hand neighbour with another stitch in the same way. Give the smocking the occasional pull from top to bottom to regulate the gathers.

4 On the next and other second rows, turn the work so you are still smocking from left to right. Treat the dots in the upper row as normal. On the lower (already gathered) row, pick up each left-hand fold, then make a small stitch over both folds close to the one below.
Bring the needle out between the two folds before picking up the next upper row dot.

Below: A fresh look for a pair of blouses – choose a matching embroidery thread for mock smocking on collars and cuffs.

Crisply smocked collars and cuffs

Give a touch of originality to a blouse already in your wardrobe or adapt a classical blouse pattern with the addition of a fresh white lawn smocked collar and cuffs.
The quick mock smocking technique is ideal for both these projects because it produces a neat frill.

Changing a plain collar

Here's how to transform a plain ready-made blouse into something special. Just remove the original collar and replace it with a smocked frill.

You will need

Blouse with regular or tab collar
10cm/⅛yd white cotton lawn (width 90cm/36in)
1 skein Coats Anchor coton à broder or stranded cotton to match blouse
5cm/2in-wide light iron-on Vilene
White sewing thread
Smocking dots size G transfer *or* one sheet each of tracing paper and dressmaker's carbon paper
Press stud

Preparing the collar

Remove collar and collar band from blouse and measure neck edge from centre front to centre front. Cut a strip of lawn 6cm/2¼in wide and twice neck measurement plus 2cm/¾in.

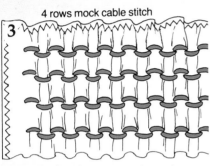

4 rows mock cable stitch

3 On the right side, working from left to right, smock four rows of mock cable stitch. Use one strand of coton à broder or three of stranded cotton. Check that collar fits neck edge.

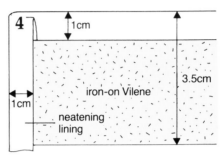

4 Cut another strip of white lawn 4.5cm/1¾in wide and the length of the smocked collar plus 2cm/1in. Interface with iron-on Vilene. Press under a 1cm/½in hem on one long edge and both short edges.

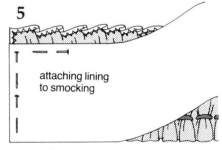

attaching lining to smocking

5 Use this strip to line the back of the smocked frill. Pin it in place with top edge level with top row of smocking and short edges flush. Machine round close to folded edges of lining strip with white thread.

Adding a smocked collar and cuffs to a classic blouse

The smart red blouse shown on the previous page is made up from a commercial paper pattern; choose one with a collar band and cuffs up to 5cm/2in wide.

You will need

Blouse pattern and fabric
40cm/½yd white cotton lawn (width 90cm/36in)
1 skein Coats Anchor coton à broder or stranded cotton to match blouse
10cm/⅛yd light iron-on Vilene
White sewing thread
Smocking dots size G transfer *or* one sheet each of tracing paper and dressmaker's carbon paper

cuffs smocked with mock surface honeycomb stitch

Collar

Cut out blouse, omitting collar, collar band and cuff pieces. Make up the blouse to the point where the collar is to be attached. Prepare the collar as for the ready-made blouse up to, and including, step 2.
On the right side, working from left to right, smock four rows of mock surface honeycomb stitch.
Make the collar band paper pattern piece smaller by pinning a fold in the centre so that finished collar band will meet at centre front and not overlap. Cut one collar band in white lawn and interface with iron-on Vilene. Press seam allowance under all round and trim to 8mm/⅜in. Complete collar as for ready-made blouse from step 5 to end, again setting collar on to neck edge so that only three rows of smocking show.
Adjust button positions so that top one lies just below upper neck edge.

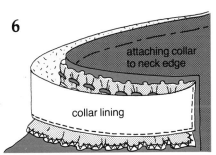

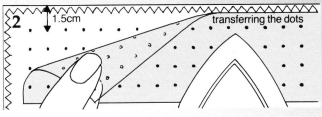

1 Press under a 1cm/½in hem on one long edge and both short edges. Neaten folded edges with a tiny zigzag machine stitch and trim off excess hem – this is the finished edge of the frill.

2 Transfer four rows of smocking dots to the right side of the lawn, either by pressing them on from a transfer or by tracing off the ones given below and transferring them with dressmaker's carbon paper. Place top row of dots 1.5cm/⅝in from the finished frill edge.

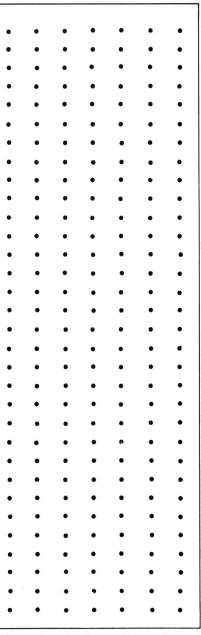

transfer dots this way up for collar and cuffs

Above: Transfer these smocking dots to the fabric with dressmaker's carbon paper. Trace them off as many times as you need to cover the length of the collar piece.

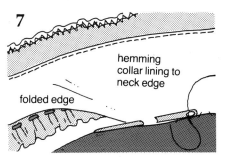

Attaching the collar

Pin collar to blouse neck edge, right sides together, taking care not to catch in collar lining strip and positioning collar so that its raw edge is flush with neck edge of blouse.

6 Tack and stitch all round between first and second rows of smocking so that only three rows show on right side.

7 Turn under raw edge of collar lining. Secure inside neck edge by hemming. Add a press stud to top of blouse opening to close (top button may have been removed with old collar).

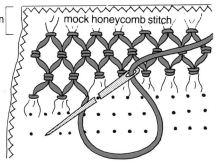

Cuffs

Using the cuff pattern piece as a guide, measure finished length and width of cuff. Cut two strips of lawn measuring this width plus 4cm/1½in by twice finished length plus 2cm/¾in. Press under a 1cm/½in hem on one long edge and both short edges. Neaten these pressed edges with a tiny zigzag and trim off excess hem – these are the finished cuff edges. On the right side, transfer the smocking dots, placing top row 1.5cm/⅝in from frill edge and bottom row not less than 1cm/½in from unfrilled edge. The number of smocking rows will depend on the cuff width.

Smock the cuff with mock surface honeycomb stitch, working from left to right. Check that smocked cuff will fit nicely round wrist with overlap for button and buttonhole. Cut two more cuff pieces in lawn. Interface with light iron-on Vilene, turn in seam allowances and trim to 8mm/⅜in. Use these to line the back of smocked cuffs. Pin in place with outer edges flush with top row of smocking. Tack and machine along short edges and outer edge.

Sew cuffs to gathered sleeve edges with right sides together, positioning cuff so that one row of smocking is caught inside the seam. Do not catch in cuff lining. Trim seam, turn in raw edge of cuff lining and slipstitch to inside of cuff. Complete blouse as given in the pattern instructions, making buttonholes as normal.

CHAPTER 19

Traditional smocking

Today's new interest in smocking means that the range of traditional patterns is expanding. Items ranging from cushions and mobiles to pretty childrens' clothes are smocked with motifs such as bears, rabbits and flower baskets, using easy stitches.

This party dress is made even prettier with smocking decoration in pastel shades of stranded cotton and three flower baskets on the front.

With real smocking, unlike mock smocking, you need to pleat (gather) the fabric before working the embroidery. Preparing pleats takes time, but it is worth doing well.

Pleating machines It is possible to obtain small machines which can automatically pleat 16 rows at the same time in 15 minutes, although these are rather expensive.

Pleating by hand

You'll need transfer dots size K for cottons and size Q for wools, strong sewing thread and a steam iron if possible. Remember to allow three times as much fabric as the width of smocking you need.

Wash and press fabric. Straighten it by tearing across the grain or pulling a thread and trimming. Cut the dots transfer to the required size – two more rows than you plan

Basic smocking stitches

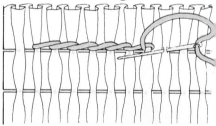

Outline stitch

Pick up a pleat just above the line of the gathering thread. Keeping the thread above the needle, make the stitch from right to left. Stitch into each successive pleat.

Deeper smocking stitches

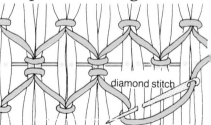

diamond stitch

Wave stitch

Work one downward cable. Keeping the thread below, move up halfway to the next gathering thread (one half space) and pick up the next pleat. Work one upward cable.

Diamond stitch Work two rows of half-space waves one above the other.

Some basic guidelines

Refer to page 80 for basic know-how and materials. Use three strands of stranded cotton on cotton fabrics and four strands of No 8 pearl cotton on wool or Viyella.

Never smock the first three and last three pleats – they serve as your seam allowance. Most stitches are worked from left to right (if right-handed).

Left handers should hold the work vertically rather than horizontally and turn stitch diagrams upside down. To begin a smocking thread, knot one end firmly. Pick up one pleat on the back of the work and come to the front through the left hand side of a pleat. To finish off, go through to the back on the right side of a pleat, then make two backstitches.

Pick up no more than a third of the depth of a pleat and always keep the needle parallel to the pleating threads. Make sure all the threads lie flat – control stranded cottons by running them over a block of beeswax. **The basic smocking stitches** are worked from left to right. None of them is very elastic. Always begin your smocking with one of these.

to smock – and transfer as described in the last chapter.

Picking up the dots Using a contrasting colour of strong thread, with a knot at one end, about 15cm/6in longer than the width of the fabric, begin picking up the dots from right to left. These threads are removed later.

When all the dots are picked up, slowly pull up the threads to form

pleats. Pull the fabric lengthwise, to make the pleats sit correctly, and steam it to set them.

Tie off the threads in pairs with an overhand knot, having all the knots in a straight line and the pleats evenly distributed. In general, the pleated fabric should be about 2.5 to 3cm/1 to 1½in narrower than the desired size, because of the elasticity of the finished smocking

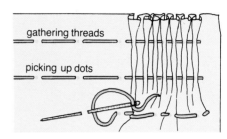

after the gathering threads have been released.

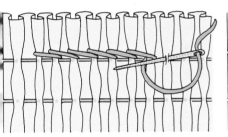

Stem stitch
Work as for outline stitch, but with the thread below the needle.

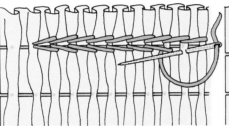

Wheat stitch
Work row of outline stitch with a row of stem stitch directly underneath. This gives a pretty effect like continuing ears of wheat.

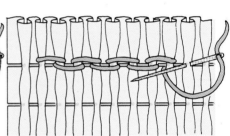

Cable stitch
Use this stitch on the back of the work where extra hold is needed. Pick up a pleat with the thread above the needle (upward cable), then pick up the next pleat with the thread below (downward cable).

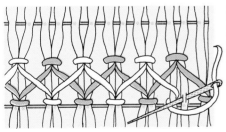

Crossed diamond stitch
Work one downward cable. Now work a half-space wave upwards and continue in wave stitch along the row. Change the colour of thread and work another row crossing the first, on the free pairs of pleats.

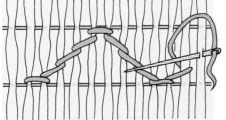

Trellis stitch
This combination of cable stitch and outline stitch is worked over the space between two pleating threads – divide the area roughly into three, by eye.

Begin with a downward cable at the

pleating thread, then work outline stitches at ⅓ the way up, ⅔ the way up, and the whole way up (just below the pleating thread).

Work an upward cable just above the pleating thread – this is the centre top stitch. Work the second to fourth stitches in reverse, with the thread above the needle to return to the bottom pleating thread. Work a downward cable stitch to match the first one.

Party dress with smocking

Smocked dresses are traditional for little girls, but here's a delightfully pretty one with flower basket motifs instead of the usual rows of cable and wave stitches.

The top and bottom border design from the front of the dress is used over the whole back yoke. If your pattern's smocked area is deeper, add extra rows of this border.

You will need

Commercial paper pattern for smock-yoked dress (the one shown here has a smocked back yoke too. If your pattern has a plain back, allow extra fabric for smocking)
Fabric and notion requirements as given on pattern envelope
Strong thread for pleating

DMC stranded cotton in greens 369 and 955, yellows 743 and 745, lilac 211, pink 899, blue 813, plus 1 skein to match fabric

Preparing to smock

When smocking a dress yoke or bodice like this one, treat the back as one piece of fabric until after working the smocking. Mark the centre back (position of back opening) and do not smock the six centre pleats. This allows space for a centre back opening and seam. Pleat 16 rows on the rectangular pieces for the front and back. Do not cut out the armholes until the smocking is completed. Pull up pleating threads to desired size.

Smocking the front

Row 1: Begin at the top with one row of wheat stitch (369).
Rows 2 to 3½: Beginning on row 2, work five cables (starting upward), one half-space wave, three cables (starting downward), one half-space wave, continue along the line (955).
Between each group of five cables and level with them, work three cables in alternating colours (745, 899 and 813). Repeat on row 3, reversing the pattern.
Rows 13½ to 15: Repeat as above, but only add the three cables on the top row of cables and waves.
Rows 9½ to 12: Work three baskets,

Chart for party dress

row 1

row 2

row 3

cable and wave border

row 4

DMC stranded cotton □ 369 ▨ 955 □ 745 ▨ 899 ▨ 813

row 9

basket

lazy daisy stitch

row 10

row 11

▨ 899 ▨ 813 ▨ 210

□ 745

row 12

□ 743

each vertical line represents one pleat

Smocked ball

This original plaything for a baby's cot is exquisitely pretty yet inexpensive to make. All you have to do is smock a length of fabric, join it into a tube, and use it to cover a child's lightweight ball.

You will need

18cm×70cm/7in×28in white cotton poplin
1.50m/1⅝yd 6mm/¼in ribbon
1 skein stranded cotton
1 foam playball

Left: Cover a lightweight ball with smocked fabric to make a delightful gift for a new baby. Stitch it in pink, as shown here, or blue.

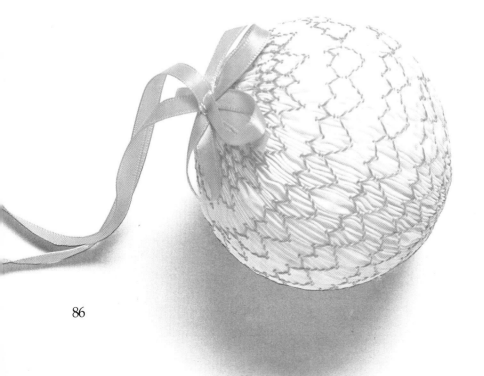

centring them by counting pleats. The top row of each basket is five crossed diamonds in 745 and 743. Reduce by one wave stitch each time, turning work upside down after each row, until you have just one stitch at the base of the basket.
Flowers Using lazy daisy (detached chain) stitch (page 9), embroider five flowers above each of the baskets – two pink, two blue and one lilac. Work the petal catching stitches through the peaks of the pleats.
Rows 6 to 13: Smock on the reverse side with cable stitch to match fabric.

Smocking the back
Remember to leave the six centre pleats empty.
Rows 2 to 14½: Work as for front borders (form double rows).
On back, smock one row of cable stitch at row 2½.

Making up
Oversew (or machine zigzag) along top and bottom edges of smocked rectangles. Follow pattern instructions for remainder of cutting out and making up. Remove pleating threads.

Right: You don't have to smock the back of the dress as well, but it does look enchanting. The cable and wave border design is used throughout.

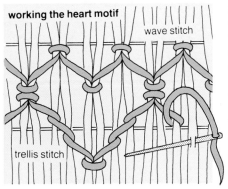

working the heart motif
wave stitch
trellis stitch

Working the smocking
Pleat 16 rows. Rows 1 and 16 are not smocked, these threads are used to pull the ends together for mounting and making up. Work in heart motif on rows two to 14.
To form heart motif, work one row

of half-space wave stitch. Beneath the downward cables of this row, work a full-space row of trellis stitch, so that every upward point of the trellis lies close to every alternate downward cable of the wave stitch.
On row 15, work cable stitch. When the smocking is completed, pull out all the gathering threads except the first and last. Slipstitch ends of fabric together to form a tube, and insert the foam ball.

Making up
Pull the two gathering threads to enclose the ball and trim fabric edges so they do not overlap. Work white tacking stitches over both ends to make fabric lie as flat as

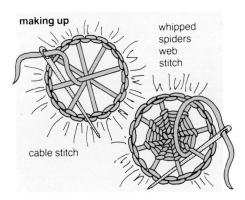

making up
whipped spiders web stitch
cable stitch

possible.
Cover these raw ends with a whipped spider's web embroidery stitch (see diagram).
Make a rosette bow with the ribbon; make a large loop and stitch to one end of ball.

CHAPTER 20

Tambour beadwork

*Try this method of attaching decorative beads to fabric
using a hook instead of a sewing neeale.
With practice, it soon becomes a quick technique, suitable
for adding glamour to evening wear and accessories,
like the silk scarf shown in this chapter.*

Tambour embroidery (threadwork without beads) originated in the Orient and was used a lot in Europe between 1780 and 1850 when many dresses and accessories were tamboured. The fabric was stretched in a circular tambour frame (so called because it resembled a drum), so tambour embroidery got its name from the frame it was worked in. Tambour beading appears to have originated in Luneville, France in 1878.

Equipment for tambouring

Apart from the beads themselves and the thread to secure them, the two main pieces of equipment you need are a frame and a special hook.

Frame The fabric must be stretched taut in a supported frame, leaving both hands free for working. A ring frame with a table clamp is suitable if the whole design to be beaded will fit inside it, leaving a margin all round for ease of working. If the design is larger, use a supported rectangular (slate) frame.

Tambour hook The tambour hook is like a very fine crochet hook. It is held in a wooden holder by means of a screw. The hook is inserted into the

Tambouring techniques

Work with the design marked on the wrong side of the fabric, which is mounted in the frame with the wrong side uppermost.
When working the tambour stitch, a chain stitch forms on the upper surface and a backstitch forms on the underside holding each bead.

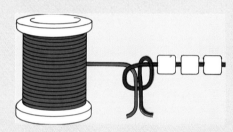

Threading the beads

First thread the beads you need on to the reel of working thread. If the beads are pre-strung, make a weaver's knot with the beads' thread and the working thread and slide the beads across on to the working thread.

Basic stitching technique

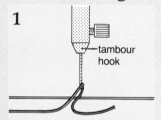
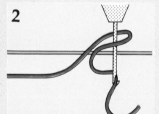
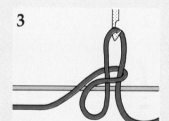
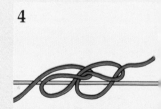

1 **2** **3** **4**

How to begin (without beads)
With the fabric mounted in the frame, wrong side up, work on the wrong side, from left to right.

1 Insert the hook in the fabric, pick up a loop of thread and pull through.
2 Twisting the hook (one half-turn), re-insert it to the right of this loop,

pick up a loop from the loose end and twist the hook again, maintaining tension.
3 Bring this loop up through the fabric, and

repeat step 2.
4 Pull the loose end of thread up through the fabric.

Finishing off

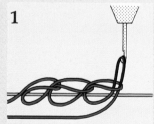
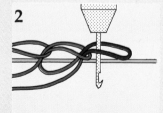
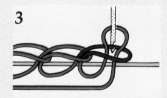
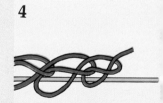

1 **2** **3** **4**

1 Pull a loop through as if making a stitch.

2 Re-insert the hook, almost in the same hole, but leaving the first loop loose.

3 Pull the second loop through the first loop and remove hook. Cut thread beneath fabric.

4 Pull second loop to bring cut end through. Tighten and cut off neatly.

holder so that it faces in the same direction as the screw. So you always know which way it is facing when it is in the fabric.

Materials for beadwork

You're likely to be working on a very special 'heirloom' piece, so it's worth choosing good materials.

Fabrics A transparent fabric such as organdie is a good choice to start on, as the beads are applied to the underside of the fabric and so can be seen when working. Firmly-woven fabric can, of course, also be used.

The weight of the fabric should be judged according to how solid the beadwork is going to be, as beads become quite heavy when packed close together. If the fabric was not heavy enough to support it, this could spoil the hang of a garment. In extreme cases, the weight of the beads could tear the fabric.

Thread The working thread should be a smooth, strong thread like Sylko or Gütermann pure silk which either matches the base fabric or forms a contrast. Gold and silver threads are effective, either on their own or with beads used every other stitch. Metallic threads must also be smooth and strong.

Beads There is a large range of colours and shapes available in beads, sequins and bugle beads.

Some are pre-threaded, others you will have to thread up yourself.

Designs

Linear designs are best for tambour beadwork. It is much quicker to work reasonably long lines of beading than having to keep starting and finishing in a design of mainly short lines. Tambour beading becomes very quick with practice and that is why it is the method used for most commercial beadwork. Sequins and bugle beads can also be attached by this method, and the stitch can also be used on its own for decorative effects, particularly with gold or silver thread.

If the beads are loose, thread them on to the working thread using a beading needle.

If possible, place the reel of thread on a peg (a blunt nail is useful for this) in one of the holes on the embroidery frame. (The thread must be free-running.)

Hold the tambour hook in the right hand above the frame and the thread in the left hand below the frame, and follow the diagrams for anchoring the thread, working the stitch and securing the thread at the end of the line of stitching. It is a good idea to practise stitching

without beads until you have mastered the use of the hook.

To attach beads, push one bead up close to the fabric before the thread is wrapped around the hook to make the stitch and repeat this on every stitch for a solid line, or every other stitch for a speckled effect.

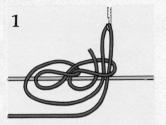

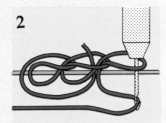

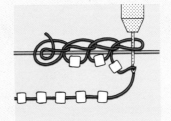

a selection of threads, beads, sequins and tambour hook for tambour beadwork

Continuous stitching
Repeat these steps following design lines.
1 Insert hook, pick up loop of thread and twist hook. Pull loop through.

2 Twist the hook, then re-insert it to the right of where the loop came through (make stitch length as required). Pick up another loop.

Stitching with beads
Push one bead up to the fabric with the left hand before the thread is twisted round the hook, then work the stitch.

Sparkling beaded evening scarf

This beautiful beadwork design is really effective. You don't have to use the beadwork on both ends of the scarf and if you prefer, stitch them down using a beading needle.

You could use this design to give a sparkle to evening bags, a silk camisole, or even jacket pockets. The shade numbers of beads used here are given in brackets, but pick them to tone with the scarf fabric.

You will need
0.80m/⅞yd Thai silk fabric (width 1m/40in)
2 reels Gütermann silk thread to match fabric
1 reel Rexor gold thread
2,000 turquoise glass tube beads
59g round beads (half each in shades of yellow and dull gold)
1,000 3mm/⅛in gold sequins
Embroidery slate frame

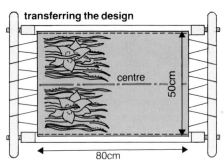

transferring the design

centre

50cm

80cm

Preparing the fabric
Cut the piece of fabric in half lengthwise and frame up one of the pieces wrong side uppermost, straight grain running horizontally. The other piece is used for backing. Run a line of tacking along the centre of the fabric, dividing it in two horizontally.
Transfer the design twice (if working both ends of scarf), centring it in each half of the framed fabric and having the lower edge of the design 5cm/2in from the raw ends.

Working the design
Following the colour key, bead the two designs as described earlier. Solid lines denote a bead on every stitch. Dotted lines should be beaded every other stitch and random dots show where you should sew the beads at random.

Making up the scarf
When the beadwork is complete, take the fabric off the frame and cut in half along tacking line. Thread the machine with the silk thread used for the beading. Stitch together the two short edges at opposite ends to the beadwork with right sides facing, taking 1cm/½in seams.
To back the scarf, cut the remaining piece of fabric in half lengthwise and machine two of the short edges together as for the scarf front. Press both seams open and place the beaded piece and the backing right sides together. Stitch all round, leaving about 10cm/4in unstitched. Turn to the right side through this opening and slipstitch closed. Press seamed edges carefully.

Left: Beadwork transforms a silk scarf.

Trace pattern for beaded scarf

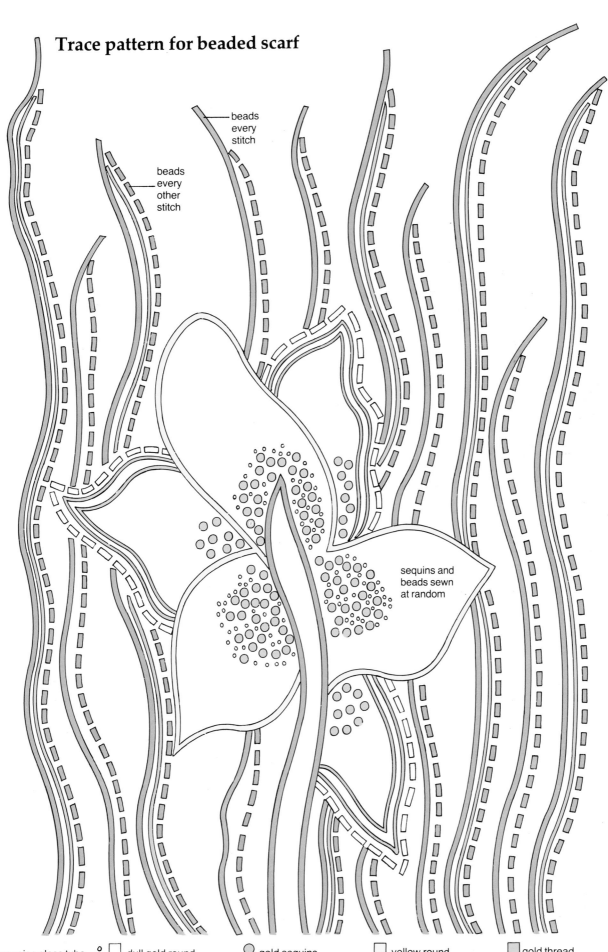

beads
every
stitch

beads
every
other
stitch

sequins and
beads sewn
at random

turquoise glass tube
beads attached with
matching thread

dull gold round
beads attached with
gold thread

gold sequins
attached with
gold thread

yellow round
beads attached with
matching thread

gold thread

CHAPTER 21

Exquisite gold and silver thread work

Gold threadwork in embroidery is not reserved for coronation robes or regimental regalia. It is simple to do and the effect is glorious. Choose from a range of real or imitation gold or silver threads to stitch something really special.

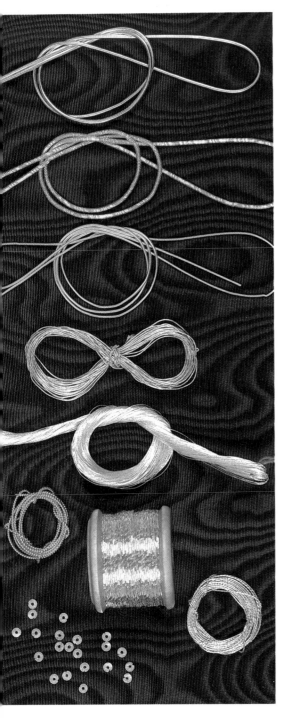

Left: A selection of materials commonly used for goldwork. Gold purl is usually sold in lengths varying from 30cm/12in to 122cm/48in. Other items come on reels or in skeins.
From top to bottom: Bright bullion No 1, bright check purl No 1, rough gold No 6, gold passing No 5, Danish silver, imitation gold Jap, gold pearl purl No 1, silver Lumi yarn No 8, gold spangles.

Goldwork is one of the most luxurious forms of embroidery. Being one of the most expensive, it has traditionally been reserved for ecclesiastical and regimental purposes, but today, you can combine small quantities of gold thread with less expensive imitation threads to create rich effects.

The earliest examples of gold embroidery come from China and Japan – embroiderers used small strips of gold wound around a silken core. Byzantine textiles often included gold embroidery on robes and between 900 and 1500AD England became famous for *Opus Anglicanum* (English work), usually executed by men, in London, using silk and metal threads on church vestments. The backgrounds to these designs were filled with vast amounts of gold couching (gold thread caught on the fabric surface with small stitches). Between the Middle Ages and the 17th century, *or nué* became popular – a technique of couching gold with coloured silks to make a shaded pattern on the gold. Western Europe led the world in goldwork in the 17th and early 18th centuries and gold embroidery for the church was revived in England in the 19th century, but it was not until this century that any amount was done in people's homes.

Types of thread for goldwork

Japanese gold (Jap) is one of the most useful and in its genuine form it is gold leaf burnished on to narrow strips of paper, lightly wound around a silk core. This is not always easy to obtain, and an imitation Jap made of lurex is suitable. Alternatives are twisted gold cord, and passing (metal threads spun round a central cotton or silk filament) which can be used doubled for extra thickness.

Gold purl, sold by weight, is a soft metal spring which is cut to the length of the stitch, threaded on the needle and sewn down like a bead. Different qualities are available, such as rough (a dull spring), smooth (a shiny spring) and bright check (a more sparkly, crinkled spring). Pieces of gold purl are known as 'chips'. There is a coarser version of purl, known as bullion.

Pearl purl is a rigid spring which looks like a string of tiny beads and comes in different sizes. It should be very slightly stretched before couching (catching down on the fabric) to allow the stitches to slip down between the coils. The thread is invisible on the finished work.

Spangles are like gold sequins, but each has a slit in it, making it more malleable over a padded or moulded surface.

Many of these items (or their equivalents) are available in silver – real or imitation – so you can create similar effects in silver.

The techniques of goldwork

Keep and cut the gold purl on a cutting board or a piece of felt. Use an old pair of scissors to cut the metal.

The fabric to be embroidered must always be mounted on a frame and also on to a backing fabric – usually holland (duck linen). This is because goldwork needs a strong foundation. The threads are heavy and need as much support as possible.

There are several different ways of working gold embroidery, but all of them consist of applying the gold or silver to the surface of the ground fabric with *couching* stitches to hold it in place. The couching is done with a double yellow polyester thread although traditionally a waxed silk Maltese thread was used.

Types of goldwork

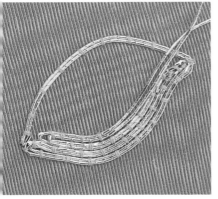

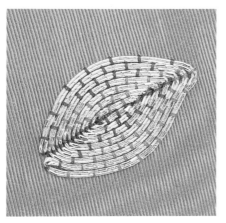

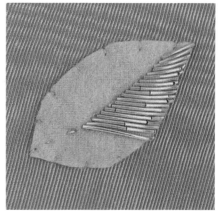

Couched gold thread can be used in a single line only, to outline work, or in flat goldwork, where shapes or background areas are filled in with solid gold couching, using a matching yellow thread.

Or nué In this type of flat goldwork, the effect is provided by the couching threads which are usually coloured and spaced out in various ways to make a shaded pattern over the gold.

Padded goldwork Padding gives a raised effect which emphasises parts of the design. To pad out a shaped, non-linear motif, cut pieces of yellow felt in the shape of the motif and stitch them in place using yellow thread.
Now work the gold embroidery over the felt, completely covering it.

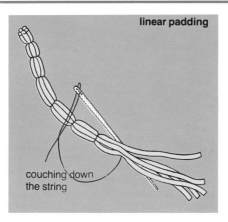

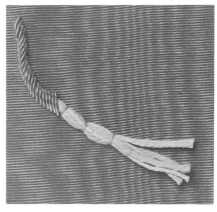

Linear padding To pad linear parts of a design – making raised flower stems for instance – use fine string, which has been drawn over beeswax to strengthen it.
Couch the string down along the design line using as many thicknesses of string as you need. Work the couching, bringing the needle up and down at the same point each time.
Cover the string with purl chips. Bring the couching thread through from the back at the end. Thread a purl chip on the needle and stitch it in place so that it lies diagonally across the string and close to the fabric at either end. Work along the

stem or line, bringing the needle up at the left and tucking it down on the right, beneath the stitch above. Use a fingertip to smooth chips.

Above: A padded line being worked over with rough gold purl chips.
Below: You could stitch any simple design on this envelope-shape bag.

Evening bag with gold embroidery

This simple, but smart evening clutch bag (14cm × 21cm/5½in × 8½in) has an exquisite gold design of a thrush perched on a rose branch. The bird and leaves gleam with a lustre that is unique to goldwork and the simple design provides you with an opportunity to explore some of the basic techniques involved in this fascinating craft.

You will need
½m/½yd furnishing fabric, moiré, velvet or silk (any width)
½m/½yd holland (duck linen)
25cm/¼yd medium interfacing
25cm/¼yd 2-3oz polyester wadding
Small piece of yellow felt
Button or press stud
1 reel Japanese gold, size 12 or smaller
About 45cm/18in each of purl in rough, smooth, check and bright check
About 25cm/10in of pearl purl
1 spangle
Yellow polyester sewing thread
Fine needle for stitching down purl
Rectangular embroidery frame
Large chenille needle

Mounting the fabric

Trim the piece of top fabric to 25cm × 50cm/10in × 20in and trim the piece of holland backing to 35cm × 50cm/14in × 20in.

To mark the bag stitching line on to the fabric, using the dimensions given in the diagram, make a paper template, pin to the fabric and run a line of tacking all round the edge. Mount the holland on a rectangular frame and then mount the fabric on the holland with the flap portion placed as centrally as possible. Oversew, beginning at the centre of each side in turn, so that no wrinkles occur. Tighten up the frame. Now trace and transfer the bird design to the centre of the bag using the trace and tack method given on page 10.

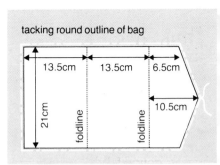

tacking round outline of bag

13.5cm   13.5cm   6.5cm

21cm   foldline   foldline   10.5cm

Stitching the goldwork design

Trace off wing and leaf shapes from the pattern, then cut them out in yellow felt, and stitch them in place on the fabric as a light padding, using yellow thread.

Use the diagram showing the position of the different materials to work the gold embroidery.

Cut a length of Jap gold about 90cm/36in long and fold it in half. Catch the loop down about halfway along the bird's back and continue catching the doubled thread down at about 4mm/⅛-¼in, outlining the head and underside of the wing. Return along the lower edge of the wing, spacing the stitches alternately with those in the row below to make a bricklike effect. Fill in the whole wing, and when you get near the top, run a row round under the upper wing outline. This makes it easier to conceal the thread ends. Two stitches away from the end, take the ends of Jap gold down through the fabric using the chenille needle, then work the last two couching stitches. This method will disturb the gold as little as possible. Fasten the ends of the Jap into the

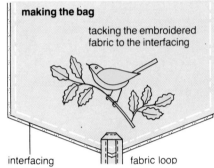

making the bag

tacking the embroidered fabric to the interfacing

interfacing   fabric loop

back of the work.

Couch the main part of the stem and the bird's tail in the same way. Add thorns to the stem, and work the bird's downy underside using chips of rough purl. Use a spangle and a chip for the eye and a check purl chip for the beak. The legs are of pearl purl – bend two pieces over the branch for feet.

Lay purl chips over the felt for the leaves, using a different type for each side of a leaf to suggest the play of light on the leaves. Vary the length for a feathery effect, covering the felt completely.

Lastly, add a length of pearl purl down the centre of each leaf.

finishing off   fold

fold

Making the bag

Remove the work from the frame and cut out the bag shape, 1.5cm/⅝in outside the tacked seamlines, to allow for seams. Cut another piece of the same fabric to the same size for lining.

Tack the wrong side of the embroidered piece to interfacing and trim edges flush. Place lining fabric and wadding together, tack round edge and trim evenly.

To make a button fastening, position a small fabric loop on the right side of the embroidered flap, with folded end pointing towards the embroidery.

Place lining and embroidery with right sides together, pin and tack round the edges. Stitch all round with a 1.5cm/⅝in seam, leaving top straight edge open. Clip corners and trim wadding and interfacing close to seam line. Remove tacking.

Finishing off

Turn bag to right side, turn in seam allowance and topstitch opening. Fold up bag front and topstitch the sides together and continue stitching round the flap. Fold flap down and attach button or press stud to close.

Right: Black and gold is a stunning combination, but you may prefer a colour to match a special outfit.

Trace pattern for goldwork bird

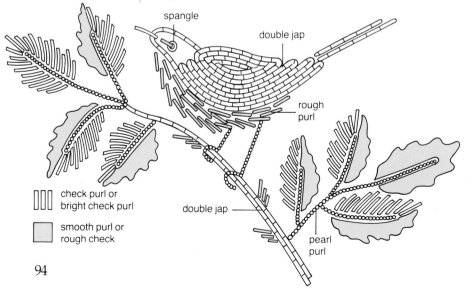

spangle

double jap

rough purl

double jap

pearl purl

check purl or bright check purl

smooth purl or rough check

Trinket box lid

Take the thrush motif from the
evening bag design and embroider
it in silver for the top of a silver
trinket box. Use silver imitation Jap,
and silver-plated smooth and bright
check purl, couched and stitched in
grey thread. Choose moiré or satin
for the ground fabric.

Index